LONG
LIVE THE
QUEEN!

Visit **LONDON** IN CORONATION YEAR

BRITISH RAILWAYS

British Railways poster showing the Horse Guards outside Buckingham Palace, 1953.

LONG
LIVE THE
QUEEN!

BRITAIN IN
1953

PETER STREET

SUTTON PUBLISHING

First Published in 2003 by
Sutton Publishing Limited · Phoenix Mill
Thrupp · Stroud · Gloucestershire ·GL5 2BU

British Library Cataloguing in Publication Data
A catalogue record for this book is available from the British Library.

ISBN 0 7509 3216 3

Typeset in 10/15 Nimrod MT.
Typesetting and origination by
Sutton Publishing Limited.
Printed in England by
J.H. Haynes & Co. Ltd, Sparkford.

Contents

J and P
unconditional love

Acknowledgements

This book would not have been possible without the help and support of many people, including family, friends and students who were willing to be questioned on life during 1953, recall their memories and unearth memorabilia of that year. I would also like to thank the staff of the British Library and University of London Library, as well as the staff of St Ives (Cornwall), Swindon and Torquay libraries. A special thanks to Ms J. Vesey and staff at Sutton Publishing for their part in this venture.

Picture research – Image Select International. All pictures, unless otherwise stated, courtesy of Topham Picturepoint.

Fashionable fare: full poplin skirt with big pockets and blouse.

Good Morning, 1953

The New Year and the young Queen were cheered as Big Ben struck midnight on the last day of December 1952. The crowds in Trafalgar Square gathered around the huge Christmas tree given by Norway, or else near – indeed sometimes in – the floodlit fountains. Across the way there was singing and dancing near the church of St Martin-in-the-Fields while fireworks in Piccadilly Circus saw in 1953 with a bang. Here people celebrated the occasion by wearing paper hats, masks, national dress or fancy costumes. Members of the United States Air Force were very much in evidence. Led by black American musicians many in the area formed a conga; others began singing 'God Save the Queen!' Not too far away, in the Royal Albert Hall, the Chelsea Arts Ball, complete with the Dagenham Girl Pipers, had taken 'Happy and Glorious' as its theme. The greater abundance now of material meant that the displays much exceeded those of recent years. High above the crowd there, and draped with crimson cloth, were four golden crowns. There was also a tapestry that showed, in brilliant colours, the Lion of England and the Unicorn of Scotland 'fighting for the crown'. But the focus of attention was a medieval arch that came to life at midnight, the central pinnacle rising to reveal a tinselled sculpture of a woman. Midnight at the ball was marked by the release of innumerable balloons and 5,000 people cheering for the year and the Coronation that lay ahead.

Throughout the country people marked the dawn of 1953. In Torquay dancers at the Marine Spa were similarly showered in balloons at the appropriate time and guests at the Grand Hotel celebrated until 2 a.m. When they eventually roused themselves the following day, the

New Year's Eve celebrations in Trafalgar Square, 1950s.

holly, mistletoe and other Christmas decorations had been replaced by fragrant spring flowers. But the religious significance of the moment was not neglected either. Several watch-night services, often particularly well attended, took place throughout the land. People seemed determined to mark the birth of a new year and the dawning of what many called the 'new Elizabethan age'.

For others, however, New Year's Eve had already proved memorable, notably for Walter Midgley while performing in *Rigoletto* at the Royal Opera House, Covent Garden, on the last night of the old year. During the first act, when he was singing the aria 'Questa a quella', his false moustache slipped into his throat and he swallowed it. He stopped singing, turned his back on the audience and made a (failed) attempt to retrieve it. He resumed the aria but in a rather more restrained way. It was not until New Year's Day that a doctor removed the final piece of nylon gauze.

For most people in England and Wales, Thursday 1 January was a normal working day. Certainly it was so for Mrs Caroline Mary Beale. She always rose at seven o'clock and this had been true even on her birthday, celebrated two days earlier – her 104th. Therefore, while many people might stay up until midnight to 'see in the New Year' and toast it accordingly, celebrations were short-lived and sleep essential. Within a few hours they might have to make their way to factory, mill, office or shop. Many walked; others cycled or used public transport. Comparatively few drove, although an increasing number owned motorcycles. The bicycle was still *the* most popular form of personal transport, and many employers provided racks or sheds where they could be left.

For others an early start was also necessary, but for a different reason – New Year's Day could mean the start of the January sales. In Torquay there was around 40 per cent off Portadyne fully automatic radiograms. Normally priced at 65 guineas, a 'limited quantity' of them was now on sale for 39½ guineas. Buying on hire purchase would raise the price to 45 guineas. In London, shoppers seemed to prefer the more expensive clothes which had been marked down rather than those at what were described as 'rock-bottom' prices. Glamorous clothes, especially furs, were much in demand in preparation for the anticipated coronation parties.

Commerce and coronation tie-ins were widespread from early 1953.

Issued in
commemoration
of
Coronation Day 1953

BY

Hercules

THE FINEST BICYCLE BUILT TO-DAY

See Britain's finest range of bicycles at
your local Hercules Dealers.

"Wonder Wheels" 24-page full colour catalogue
available on request to DEPT. D.S.
THE HERCULES CYCLE AND MOTOR CO. LTD.,
ASTON, BIRMINGHAM 6

Beaver lamb coats retailed at £24, rabbit fur ('coney') coats sold at £17. Some of the stock on sale was cheaper because it had been soiled by the great smog of the previous month. One store offered 100 pairs of coloured slacks at 2s 6d each. They were all sold within 30 minutes.

For both girls (despite the name) and boys there was the chance to visit the Schoolboys' Own Exhibition in London, which had been opened the day before by the radio star Wilfred Pickles. It was a recruitment fair for those about to leave school. Modern technology seemed to arouse a great deal of interest among all those present. Displays included a model of a centurion tank and a mock-up of a modern British Railways engine, together with a demonstration of how to drive one. There was also the chance to learn how to navigate a tanker, as well as inter-planetary voyages, particularly to the moon. But if this 'supersonic world' (a term already in use at this time) was too much for some, there was always the chance to sit on a stool and practise milking on a model udder.

It's RAYON this year!

London's leading fashion designers choose the new rayons Because of the variety and appeal of this season's new rayons, London's "top eleven" designers—members of the exclusive Incorporated Society of London Fashion Designers—have all featured rayon in their Spring Collections. You can see the new rayon fabrics in the shops now — sheers, satins, taffetas, brocades and crêpes, as well as tropical-weight suitings, by the yard or made-up by the leading makers.

Here is a wonderful evening dress created by Hardy Amies in a new rayon called 'Chamba Lamé'. The halter neckline and tailored bodice form a dramatic contrast with the back-sweeping skirt. Hardy Amies, founder member of the Incorporated Society of London Fashion Designers is also adviser to a School for Fashion Careers in New York. The clothes he designs are notable for their youthful sophistication.

This rayon brocade, woven with gold and silver thread, is made by the West Cumberland Silk Mills Ltd.

THE BRITISH RAYON AND SYNTHETIC FIBRES FEDERATION
HAMILTON HOUSE, 138, PICCADILLY, LONDON, W.1

FRONT-PAGE NEWS

There were ten national newspapers in January 1953. *The Times*, priced 4d, still carried advertisements on its front page alongside such announcements as births, marriages, anniversaries and deaths. Public appointments also featured there. On 1 January Dr Barnardo's Homes (later to be renamed Barnardo's) advertised for a child welfare visitor, making clear that only women should apply. Similarly, an anonymous Midlands county town sought a 'lady clerk' for trust work. Such gender specification was perfectly legal at this

Charities and other organisations also hoped to benefit from being linked with the coronation.

time. The Colonial Service's advertisement for an architect in Northern Rhodesia (later Zambia) similarly presumed that only males would apply. Furthermore, a 'cheerful cook general' was required by a family of four who lived near Egham in Surrey; the advertisement added that there was 'no objection to a foreigner' provided that the person concerned was willing. Another domestic vacancy stated that applications from pensioners were 'acceptable'.

Given the time of the year, however, Thomas Cook was offering readers the chance to enjoy 'winter sunshine' and 'sea voyaging' to Halifax, Nova Scotia and New York. Fares started at £47 10s. The Ellerman line announced that the maiden voyage of *The City of Port Elizabeth* on 10 January was fully booked although there were vacancies on that of *The City of Exeter* (4 June). Taking 18 days to Singapore, the liner would also visit Egypt, Sumatra and Java.

Those eager to live on the English Riviera had a chance to buy a small residential estate of 185 acres with house, four miles from the coast. The accommodation comprised five reception rooms, ten main bedrooms, two bathrooms, a garage for three cars and a stall for twelve cows. All this was for £6,000.

For those who wished to remain in or were confined to their own homes, there was shopping by post. Among the items featured on New Year's Day were one-pound (weight) tins of stewed steak and onion. Eight such tins cost 30s. Twelve pounds of Devon honey could be bought for 60s; six pounds cost 32s. But perhaps the most enticing were chocolates (still rationed until early February). Maison Robert would send two pounds of chocolates at 6s 2d per pound in exchange for one pound of sugar. No coupons were required, only a postal order and the sugar. Clothes were the other major item available in this way. Advertisements ranged from home-knitted garments and tropical linen suits (at 12 guineas from a company in Maidenhead) to corsets which could be repaired and copied by Mme Mautner of Edgware, north London; outsize was her speciality.

People could also purchase boxes of violets and anemones from Lelant, Cornwall, or have delivered the 'Straight Jane mop', which was self-wringing. According to this advertisement, 'a twist of the wrist and it's wrung'. It went on to point out that no special pail was required and the mop cost £1 4s 6d. Finally, nutty slack coal was being advertised at £1 per ton.

NEWLY HONOURED

The Queen's first New Year's Honours were listed in this issue of *The Times* in full and were quite extensive, in part because they were worldwide. The Colonial Office, Commonwealth Relations

Office and Foreign Office each had its own list, as did Australia, New Zealand, Ceylon (later renamed Sri Lanka) and Pakistan. There were also awards for military service in Japan and the Korean War (still being fought at this time).

Among those honoured were Arthur ('Bomber') Harris, who had been Commander-in-Chief of Bomber Command between 1942 and 1945. He was made a baronet. Ernest Gowers, the writer and administrator, was knighted. His book *The Complete Plain Words*, had first appeared in a different form a few years earlier. The honour, however, was in recognition of wartime service as London Regional Commissioner for Civil Defence in the Second World War and as chairman of many committees and commissions, notably that on capital punishment, which was to report later in 1953. Lincoln Evans, General Secretary of the Iron and Steel Trades Confederation, and Harold Nicolson, biographer of King George V, were also knighted.

Wilder Graves Penfield, the Canadian neurologist and cytologist, was awarded the Order of Merit – an honour limited to twenty-four members and which had been instituted by King Edward VII in June 1902. It was and still is for civilians, confined to those who have advanced art, literature or science. E.M. Forster, writer of such celebrated works as *Passage to India* and *Howard's End*, was made a Companion of Honour. Kathleen Ferrier, the concert and opera singer, and Diana Wyngard, the stage and screen actress (notably in *Cavalcade* and *Gaslight*), were both awarded the CBE.

Seeing and celebrating the coronation in style.

OTHER STORIES

No particular story dominated the domestic news headlines, but there was some anxiety about the behaviour of modern youth and the quality of education that they received. The retiring address of the Revd Sir Herbert Dunnico, a magistrate at the courts of Stratford, east London, since 1920 and chairman of the juvenile court and probation committee, said he had 'fear when contemplating the future'. For too many of those who had appeared

THE

BRIGHTON BELLE

WEEKDAYS

LONDON (VICTORIA)	dep	11	0 am	3	0 pm	7	0 pm
BRIGHTON	arr	12	noon	4	0 pm	8	0 pm
BRIGHTON	dep	1	25 pm	5	25 pm	8	25 pm
LONDON (VICTORIA)	arr	2	25 pm	6	25 pm	9	25 pm

SUNDAYS

LONDON (VICTORIA)		dep	11	0 am	7	0 pm
BRIGHTON		arr	12	noon	8	0 pm
BRIGHTON		dep	5	25 pm	8	25 pm
LONDON (VICTORIA)		arr	6	25 pm	9	25 pm

BRITISH RAILWAYS

London–Brighton in an hour: celebrating twenty years as an electric train service.

before him, 'film stars and gangsters were their only god'. The availability of coshes and knuckle-dusters, he argued, encouraged amateur criminals; personal integrity, honest work and straight dealing were in decline, especially with the law being more sympathetic to the criminal than to the community. He was particularly critical of schools and their failure to impress on their pupils moral, religious and ethical values. They were even failing in their formal role as educator – so many fifteen-year-olds appearing before him had been unable to read the oath.

Concern over juveniles and their attendance at court also appeared among *The Times*' letters. One writer urged that working fathers of such young people should also be required to attend court. He observed that time off was 'frequently taken for weddings, funerals, even football matches', but that fathers seemed incapable of coming to court when their sons appeared. He acknowledged that enforcing such attendance would entail 'inevitable loss of pay (and perhaps of face at work)'. But such a policy would, he believed, ensure greater parental responsibility.

The youth of two elderly people, one of whom had just died, was also recalled in the newspaper. Mrs Jemima Greenfield, a pensioner of the News Vendors' Association, was 100 that day. As a young girl she had served Charles Dickens in her uncle's coffee house off the Strand in London. The newspaper also informed its readers that Mrs Frances Wainwright had died on New Year's Eve. Aged 106, she recalled visiting the Great Exhibition of 1851. Such an event had celebrated science's achievements at that time. But in his inaugural speech in 1953 as 114th President of the British Association for the Advancement of Science, Sir Edward Appleton, referred to the public's 'embarrassingly implicit faith in the scientist'. He thought that present-day science was too serious to be left just to scientists. The main preoccupations of overseas news (recorded under the section entitled 'Imperial and foreign news') centred around preparations in Washington for the inauguration of President Eisenhower later that month, the Mau Mau in Kenya and continuing attacks on British interests in Malaysia and Egypt.

The main features on the sports page were racing at Newbury and the conclusion of the Davis Cup challenge round in Australia. There were also details of forthcoming FA Cup matches. Such matches at this time of the year were either morning or afternoon fixtures – the Football Association would not allow such contests to take place under floodlights. Among the matches to be played was that between Preston North End and Blackpool (the eventual winner of the 1953 FA Cup Final).

Two of the characters from *The Archers* making a recording for their popular series at Broadcasting House. On the left is Tom Forrest (Bob Arnold), and on the right Widow Turvey (Courtney Hope).

TO-DAY'S TELEVISION

3.15 — Victory at Sea: 23 — Target Suribachi. 3.45—"Hill Sheep Farm" (film). 4-4.15—Watch with Mother. 5-5.55—Children: Prudence Kitten (with Annette Mills); Impressions of the Coronation—Children from the Commonwealth talk to Barbara MacFadyean; Caribbean Carnival. 8—Newsreel. 8.30 — Desmond Walter-Ellis in "Reggie Little at Large," by Godfrey Harrison. 3—Law and Disorder. 9—"La Même Route" (film specially written and produced in France as a tribute to Queen Elizabeth). 9.30—Alicia Markova and Harriet Cohen in Serenade for a Queen. 10.30—Coronation Ball from the Royal Ballroom, Tottenham, London. Music for dancing played by Geraldo and his Orchestra, Edmundo Ros and his Latin-American Orchestra, the Blue Rockets, the Harry Davidson Old Time Orchestra, the Billy Harrison Square Dance Band. 12 app.—Weather. news (sound only)

. . . AND RADIO

HOME 8 — News. 8.15—Hints for Housewives. 8.20 Morning Music. 9 —Piano. 9.30—Regimental mascots. 9.45—Schools. 10.15 —Service. 10.30 — Music While You Work. 11—Schools. 12—Records. 12.25—Midday Music-Hall. 12.55 — Weather. news. 1.10 — Eye-witness. 1.30 — Don Carlos Orch. 1.55—Cricket scores. 2—Schools. 3—The Royal drive through N.E. London. 3.15 — "The Importance of Being Earnest." 4.45 — Frank Sinatra (records). 5—Children. 5.55 — Weather, sport. 6.20—Calling Home. 7 — Goon Show. 7.40 — Coronation Chronicle. 8—Coronation Concert. 9—News. 9.15—Concert (cont.). 10.10—In All Directions. 10.40 — "Now It's Over . . ." Gilbert Harding. 11.10 — News.

LIGHT 9 — News. 9.10 — Forces' Choice. 9.55 Five to Ten. 10—

Organ. 10.30—Music While You Work. 11—Mrs. Dale. 11.15 — On With the Dance. 11.45 — Piano. 12 — Oscar Rabin's Band. 12.45 Concert Hour. 1.45—Listen with Mother. 2—Woman's Hour. 3—Music in the Home. 3.30—Organ. 3.45—Music While You Work. 4.15—Mrs. Dale. 4.30—Northern Orchestra. 5.30 Tip-Top Tunes. 6—Let the Bands Play. 6.30 — Flotsam's Fanfare. 6.45 —Archers. 7—News Headlines; Family Favourites. 7.25 — Sport. 7.30 — Wilfred Pickles at a Coronation Party. 8 — "Happy and Glorious." 8.45 — Lyons. 9.15—Come In and Sing. 10—News. 10.15—Take Your Partners. 11.15 — Stanley Black's Orch. 11.56 News.

THIRD 6 — String Quartet. 6.15 — Talk in French. 6.30—"The Dark-Eyed Sailor" (Ballad opera). 8—Talk. 8.45 — Liszt.

9.15—"The Quest of the Holy Grail." 10.45—Piano Trio. 11.25 — Coronation Year 1911.

REGIONS. Midland: 6.15—News, sport. 6.30 — Musical Soiree.

North: 6.15—News, sport. 6.30 — Coronation Day celebrations in the North.

N. Ireland: 6.15—News, sport. 6.30—As North.

Scottish: 11.40 — Schools. 2—Schools. 4.45 — Deanamaid Aoradh. 6.15—News, sport. 6.35 — Light Music. 10.10 —Ceilidh.

Welsh: 11—Ysgolion. 2—Schools. 6.15—News, sport. 6.45—Teulu Ty Coch. 7 — Llwybr Y Mynydd. 9.15—Tribute to H.M. The Queen. 10 — Music for two pianos.

West: 12.25—Songs and Piano. 12.45—Bath and West Show. 1.30—Maritza Players. 6.15—News, sport. 6.30—Light Music.

Radio and television programmes as advertised in the *Daily Sketch*, 3 June 1953.

BROADCASTING

Almost every home had a radio but only a small minority had a television at the start of 1953. There were three BBC national radio stations – the Home Service, the Light Programme and the Third Programme. On 1 January the Home Service broadcast for over sixteen hours (6.30 a.m. to 11 p.m.), the Light Programme for slightly fewer (9 a.m. until midnight). The Third Programme was on in the evening only, beginning at 6 o'clock.

Home Service programmes centred around music, news and variety. The station opened with records, offered *Children's Hour* at 5 p.m., and its evening listening included *Ray's a Laugh* (with Ted Ray) and *Variety Ahoy. Farming Today* was also broadcast in the evening. The Light Programme had music as its staple, with two 30-minute programmes of *Music While You Work* (at 10.30 a.m. and 3.45 p.m.). Perhaps the most popular song that day was 'Here in my heart' by Al Martino. This had topped the first British music chart, published by the *New Musical Express* in November 1952, and was still there when the new year began, although within a few days Jo Stafford would briefly hold that spot with 'You belong to me'. For those who preferred words to music, there was *Mrs Dale's Diary* at 11 a.m. and 4.15 p.m. In the evening people could listen to *The Archers* and *Educating Archie*. The Third Programme was devoted mainly to serious music and talks. That evening, as well as a concert, music by Fauré and Stravinsky was broadcast and Arnold Toynbee gave one of the Reith lectures, the subject of which was Russia. The station closed with *Tales from the Pacific Islands*. Television started at 3 p.m., but after five minutes for women and *The Flowerpot Men* for children closed down until it broadcast for children again at 5.30. *Newsreel* at 8 was followed by a play (*The Affair at Assino*) and closed with the weather and news – in sound only – at 10.30.

LONDON TONIGHT

Live theatre and music in the capital covered practically every taste. There was *The Marriage of Figaro* at the Royal Opera House, Covent Garden and *Il Trovatore* at Sadler's Wells. The Christmas season at the Royal Festival Hall alternated between *Harlequinade* and Tchaikovsky's *Nutcracker* in the afternoon and *Nutcracker* and Strauss's *Don Quixote* in the evening. *South Pacific* offered music of a different type. It had opened in 1951 with Mary Martin and Wilbur Evans. Audiences continued to be fascinated by Martin's nightly washing of her hair on stage. Another alternative was Billy Cotton and *Wonderful Time*, on offer twice that night at the Hippodrome.

Performances and actors in the capital included Jimmy Edwards, Vera Lynn and Tony Hancock in *London Laughs*; Robertson Hare in Ben Travers's *Wild Horses* and Charlie Chester and Michael Bentine in the pantomime *Jack and Jill*. At the Empress Hall was the pantomime *Jack and the Beanstalk* on ice. On a more serious note there was the contemporary dramatist Norman Hunter's *Waters of the Moon* with Edith Evans, Sybil Thorndike, Kathleen Harrison and Wendy Hillier. This was a study of a middle-class household in decline. Paul Scofield was in *Richard II*. Already well established was *The Mousetrap*, starring Richard Attenborough and Sheila Sim. Live entertainment of a different sort was provided by the three circuses then in the capital. These were in Harringay, Earl's Court and Olympia. London, too, was rich in the films it could offer on New Year's Day. These included *Limelight* with Charlie Chaplin, *Hans Christian Andersen* (Danny Kaye), *Golden Marie* (Simone Signoret), *The Man Who Watched Trains Go By* (Claude Rains), *The Snows of Kilimanjaro* (Gregory Peck) and *Quo Vadis?* (Robert Taylor and Deborah Kerr).

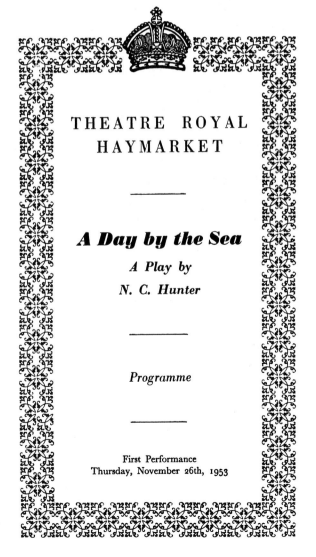

THEATRE ROYAL HAYMARKET

———

A Day by the Sea

A Play by
N. C. Hunter

———

Programme

———

First Performance
Thursday, November 26th, 1953

THE CORONATION

The Times editorial saw coronation year as 'a time of special opportunity for government and people . . . [and] greater self-reliance.' This, it argued, could best be achieved through more and better output, harder work, larger savings and wiser investment. There was only brief coverage of the anticipated event that was just over five months away. The newspaper reported that Westminster Abbey was now closed to the public until the day of the service itself (2 June). There was also a lengthy feature article on the dress requirements for those involved in the coronation ceremony.

BRITAIN IN 1953: ANALYSIS OF A NATION

According to the 1951 census, the UK population totalled some 50,210,000, with England and Wales accounting for most of it (over 87 per cent). At 550 persons per square mile in Britain as a whole, the island was one of the most densely populated areas in the world. It was also one of the most heavily urbanised. Greater London had a population of over 8.3 million people and more than 1 million lived in Birmingham and in Glasgow; there were 20 cities each with a population over 200,000. Medium-sized towns (50,000–100,000) were growing fastest and included garden cities such as Letchworth, established 50 years earlier, and new towns such as Stevenage that had been created in the postwar era.

The population was growing partly because of higher birth rates – 1947 had seen the highest such rate since 1921. It was the peak year of the baby boom (1945–55), although most families had only one or two children. The population was also rising because people were living longer and there was a net gain from international migration. Most of those leaving the UK headed for elsewhere in the British Commonwealth: Australia, Canada, New Zealand and South Africa were the most favoured destinations. The USA was also popular. Immigration was mainly by people from elsewhere in the British Empire and Commonwealth, as, following the 1948 Nationality Act, there were no restrictions on such movement and the nation's need for labour was great, especially in the public sector.

About two-thirds of the population were of working age (15–64), with about a fifth under 15 and a tenth over 65. There were slightly more females than males, a predominance that increased with age. Women outnumbered men from adolescence and there were nearly 50 per cent more women than men aged over 70. Life expectancy in England and Wales was 67 for men and 72 for women; it was about

DEATHS BY VIOLENCE

Suicide	4,758
Motor vehicle accidents	4,375
Other accidents	10,455
Homicide, operations of war	277
Total, all causes	503,523

Source: Whitaker's Almanack (1955)

two years less for both genders in Scotland. The main natural causes of death were cancer, coronary and heart disease, bronchitis, pneumonia and tuberculosis. Influenza saw a near four-fold increase from 1952 to 1953. Most deaths through violence were the result of accident. Almost 300 people in 1953 were either murdered or died in action.

There were, however, yet again more suicides than motor vehicle deaths. It was the high number of suicides (three a day in Greater London) and the absence of any help for those contemplating such action that led Chad Varah, an Anglican priest at St Stephen's Walbrook in the City, to found what became the Samaritans. He and his secretary began taking calls (telephone number MAN 9000) from 2 November 1953. Others who volunteered their help were soon organised by him and began offering advice a few months later.

While English was the predominant language in Britain, Welsh was spoken by a quarter of the population in the Principality. It was also estimated that almost 100,000 spoke Gaelic, with a particularly strong presence in Ross and Cromarty, Inverness, Argyll and Lanark. But around 2,500 spoke Gaelic only. Few now spoke the Manx and Cornish varieties of Celtic, though Irish Gaelic in Northern Ireland and French on the Channel Islands continued to be used.

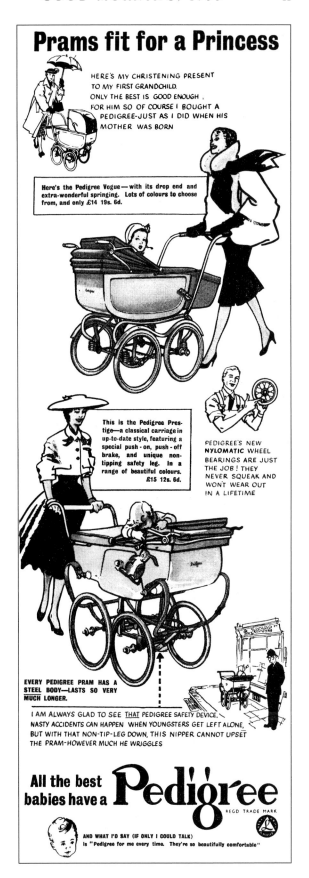

A PROMISING OUTLOOK

Over seven years after the war, Britain was a country in which war damage was still evident and smoke from steam engines, factory chimneys and home fires widespread. Although society was gradually moving away from austerity to affluence, the 'greyness of things' was still apparent to many and, in January, the rationing of meat, sugar, eggs and sweets all too real and familiar. Identity cards had been abolished in February 1952 (although their unique numbers were not discarded – they became the people's National Health Service numbers) and other things were changing as more controls on consumer goods were lightened or lifted, production increased and unemployment and inflation fell. In January 1953 Britain was the third richest country in the world and a global power with an empire (now more frequently referred to as, or linked with, commonwealth) whose head of state was to be crowned later that year.

The State of the Nation

GOVERNING THE COUNTRY

The government of the country was centred on Westminster. Although Northern Ireland had its own parliament at Stormont, there was no such regional institution in either Wales or Scotland, and only the latter had its own dedicated cabinet minister. In January, however, the Communist Party submitted evidence to the Royal Commission on Scottish Affairs arguing for a Scottish parliament and an all-party campaign for a Welsh parliament was launched in August. The country was governed by the Conservatives (led by Churchill), who had been elected in October 1951, following six years of Labour government under Clement Attlee. In a House of Commons of 625 Members of Parliament, the Conservatives had a majority of seventeen. In 1953 there were thirteen by-elections but only one seat changed hands. This was in May, when the Conservatives won Sunderland South from Labour – the first government gain in a by-election since 1924. The Speaker was W.S. ('Shakes') Morrison, a former Conservative MP, who held this position from 1951 to 1959. An MP's annual salary was £1,000 (of which £100 was allowed for expenses), together with free travel to and from the constituency. Churchill refused to allow a parliamentary select committee to consider a salary increase.

The House of Lords had around 860 members, over 800 of whom were hereditary peers, including the maximum number of sixteen from Scotland. There were also five Irish peers. This was below the number originally allocated, as vacancies from the province were no longer filled. Four Peers of the Blood, twenty-four Anglican bishops and two archbishops (Canterbury and York) were also in this chamber. Only the bishops of London, Winchester and Durham had the automatic right to a seat there, however; the remainder were appointed from those who had been bishops of their see longest. No other part of the Christian Church or other religion had the right to representation in the upper house. There were ten law lords – the only life peers at this time. It was not possible to disclaim a

Sir Anthony Eden.

hereditary peerage but at the start of each parliament peers could apply for a leave of absence. No women were allowed to sit in the Lords.

The Prime Minister was Winston Churchill. Aged seventy-eight, this was his only peacetime government. He was to be succeeded in 1955 by Sir Anthony Eden, who was Foreign Secretary (for the third time) in 1953. The colonies and the Commonwealth were each represented by a minister in the cabinet as well. R.A. ('Rab') Butler was Chancellor of the Exchequer. In April Eden was taken ill and unable to resume his duties until October, while at the end of June, following an unannounced stroke, Churchill was 'advised to rest' for some weeks. Butler took temporary charge of the government and the Marquis of Salisbury became acting Foreign Secretary.

Sir David Maxwell Fyfe was Home Secretary and Minister for Welsh Affairs. Other cabinet ministers in that year included Earl Alexander of Tunis as Minister of Defence, Harold Macmillan as Minister of Housing and Peter Thorneycroft as President of the Board of Trade. Walter Monckton was Minister of Labour and National Service (the term for conscription) and, to maintain government neutrality between capital and labour, did not attend the Conservative Party conference. The Ministers of Agriculture and Fisheries (Sir Thomas Dugdale), Education (Florence Horsbrugh, the first woman to join a Conservative cabinet) and Food (Gwilym Lloyd-George) only joined the cabinet in September 1953; the Minister of Health remained outside the cabinet throughout this year.

Those on the first steps towards a major political career in 1953 included Reginald Maudling (at this time Economic Secretary to the Treasury) and Selwyn Lloyd (Minister of State at the Foreign Office). Lord (later Sir Alec Douglas-) Home was at the Scottish Office, while Edward Heath was a junior whip. John Profumo was Parliamentary Secretary at Transport (combined with Civil Aviation from 1 October).

CHURCHILL KNIGHTED

Churchill took pride in being and remaining the 'Great Commoner'. In 1945 he had declined a knighthood of the Garter (KG). This

The future King George VI as Duke of York.

decision had disappointed King George VI and was subsequently regretted by Churchill himself. The accession of a new monarch offered the opportunity to re-issue the invitation. The Queen's Principal Private Secretary (Sir Alan Lascelles) and Churchill's (Jock Colville) discussed the matter again in 1952 and Colville raised the subject in general terms with Churchill in early 1953.

Harold Macmillan, a flamboyant and successful Minister of Housing in 1953.

Churchill was now more willing to accept the honour though still reluctant to cease being plain 'Mr Churchill'. Indeed, he told Sir Norman Brook he would have preferred to have the honour but not the change of title. Maintaining the status quo was what he wanted and in so doing he would, he joked, make it 'a discourtesy title'. Mrs Churchill was even more opposed to losing her commoner status. Only the appeal of family history – the father of his hero, the 1st Duke of Marlborough, was another Sir Winston Churchill and, as he told his doctor Charles Moran, the fact that it was now the Queen's decision alone – led to his acceptance. He dined with the Queen on 24 April and formally accepted the honour that day.

The news was well received and many wrote immediately to congratulate him. Much to his mock annoyance, though, Churchill's 'faithful chela' Viscount Brendan Bracken did not, and was 'reprimanded' by the Prime Minister accordingly. Bracken telegraphed back 'Dear Sir, recovering from shock. But give me notice of canonisation.'

CHURCHILL'S ILLNESS

Resplendent in his Garter robes on 27 May, Churchill gave a pre-coronation dinner at 10 Downing Street. The events and meetings surrounding that ceremony were almost as demanding on him as on the Queen. Indeed, he was very tired on the day itself and somewhat reluctant to attend. The following day he opened the meeting of Commonwealth Prime Ministers and on 5 June hosted, in Eden's continued absence because of ill-health, a foreign office banquet at Lancaster House. The pace rarely slackened, especially in the build-up to the Bermuda conference that had been arranged for early July. But on 23 June, towards the end of a dinner in honour of the Italian

Sir Winston Churchill leaving No. 10 Downing Street, followed by his daughter, Mrs Christopher Soames, 17 September 1953.

Prime Minister Alcide de Gasperi but unknown to those there, Churchill suffered a stroke. No ministers were told either, and the following morning Churchill insisted on presiding at cabinet, though Butler later remarked how Churchill had allowed matters to go forward without much discussion and Macmillan noticed how quiet he was on this occasion. His health worsened the next day. By 26 June his left side was partially paralysed and Charles Moran wondered whether he would survive the weekend. A press statement was issued announcing that Churchill needed a complete rest. It did not say why. Churchill initially thought that he would have to resign yet at the same time was determined to recover, and indeed did so rapidly. Within a few weeks of the stroke he was able to have visitors and returned to Downing Street in early September.

THE OPPOSITION

The Labour Party claimed in 1953 to have a membership of over 6 million if trade union and affiliated society membership were included. Individual membership totalled over 1 million and was only slightly below the peak of the previous, difficult, year. (Conservative Party membership was also at its highest in 1953 with almost 3 million.) Then the Bevanites, inspired by the former Minister of Health, had emerged, championing more socialist policies than those favoured by the party leadership. At the 1952 conference the group had won six constituency places and seemed poised to extend their argument and position in 1953. Instead a precarious balance of power was maintained and there was a marked determination to avoid quarrelling in public. The Labour Party's Annual Conference met at Margate. Its 'Challenge to Britain' was cautious in advocating further state control and disappointed many in the movement. The Bevanites retained but did not increase their representation on the executive.

The Liberal Party met at Ilfracombe under their leader Clement Davies. With only six MPs and less than 3 per cent of the votes cast in the 1951 General Election, the party was very much at the margins of the political process. It campaigned for an end to guaranteed markets and prices for agriculture, reaffirmed its faith in free trade and sought electoral reform. The Communist Party of Great Britain had lost its MPs in the 1950 General Election, experienced reduced support in that of the following year and did not hold a conference in 1953.

THE LEGISLATIVE PROGRAMME

The two principal measures of the parliamentary session concerned transport and the status of the steel industry. The Transport Act ended the obligation of the British Transport Commission (established in 1947) to integrate the nation's transport services. British Railways secured greater operating freedom (but was not to have its own board until 1962) and road haulage was returned to the private sector. The Iron and Steel Act denationalised the industry and set up the Iron and Steel Board to supervise the successor companies. Both laws were enacted in May 1953.

Perhaps the most significant legislation affecting imperial interests was the Rhodesia and Nyasaland Federation Act. This grouped the areas concerned to create the Central African Federation. Tension developed within the federation, however, especially among African nationalists. It lasted little more than ten years. In 1964 Northern Rhodesia (renamed Zambia) and Nyasaland (Malawi) became independent states within the Commonwealth.

ROYAL TITLES ACT

Elizabeth was the first British sovereign to have been specifically entitled 'Head of the Commonwealth' at her accession. The title itself had been devised and first applied to King George VI towards the end of his reign. The Royal Titles Act provided for an alteration of the royal style and titles, reflecting more clearly the actual constitutional relations of the Commonwealth members to one another and their recognition of the Crown as the symbol of their free association and of the sovereign as the head of the Commonwealth. Furthermore, it stipulated that she was Queen of each of the Commonwealth territories which were not republics (only India at the time of enactment), acting on the advice of her ministers in the different countries. Legislation on the royal title was to be passed by each country's parliament. It confirmed the divisibility of the Crown. On 29 May proclamations were issued in London, Ottawa, Canberra, Wellington, Pretoria, Colombo and Karachi giving effect to the changes as agreed by the Commonwealth governments.

AMNESTY FOR DESERTERS

Another measure occasioned by the coronation was a general amnesty to wartime deserters. Announced in February, it had been campaigned for by MPs of various parties since 1947. Under it, members of the armed forces who had deserted between 3 September 1939 and 15 August 1945 would no longer be prosecuted. Instead they were to apply for a protection certificate and would be referred to the appropriate reserve to which others had been transferred on demobilisation. The amnesty did not normally extend to other offences. Those awaiting trial or serving prison sentences for desertion would be released from custody. No precise number of those affected was available at the time of the announcement, though it was thought likely to be several thousand. The amnesty was not a precedent, and desertion continued to be a problem which was taken seriously. Since the war some ten thousand RAF men had deserted and more than half of them were still absent in February 1953.

The police had had only moderate success in their manhunts. Many deserters settled in what was now the Republic of Ireland and had made an easy return to Britain. Others began a new life under a fresh identity as civilians. Some resorted to crime. *The Times* concluded in an editorial that 'War bears unequally upon mankind,

The makers of CHURCHMAN'S No. 1 CIGARETTES

join the peoples of the Commonwealth

in saying "LONG LIVE THE QUEEN!"

and many of those who break under the strain deserve compassion even more than correction.'

FINANCE, INDUSTRY AND THE ECONOMY

The 1953 budget, Rab Butler's second, was deliberately expansionary given Treasury fears of an American recession. All rates of tax were cut by 6*d*. This meant that the standard rate was now 9*s* in the pound. Purchase tax rates were also reduced, but the tax still appeared to be applied erratically. In the area of toys, for instance, it was applied to seaside buckets but not spades, to cowboy hats but not cowboy outfits. Consumption increased in 1953 and coincided with a rise in national output of 4 per cent over the year.

The Second World War had had a tremendous adverse impact on Britain's financial and trading position, primarily because of the

The uncertain future of the British car industry: unemployed and short-time workers outside the Labour Exchange at Coventry, 1952–3.

loss of some overseas assets, new overseas debts and lost markets. Industry had had to change over from war- to peacetime output and to give priority to exports. This partly explained why restrictions remained on domestic consumption or why goods were in short supply at home in the immediate postwar period. But such restraint, although irksome, had paid off by now. In 1953 Britain's terms of trade continued to improve and its balance of payments was in surplus. Gold and dollar reserves increased in the twelve months to August by $784 million and stood at $2,456 million. The Bank rate, which stood at 4 per cent when the year opened, was reduced to 3½ per cent in September.

Some 22 million were in civil employment, of whom 4 million were in basic industry (around 700,000 in the coal industry) and nearly 9 million in manufacturing. Unemployment in August was under 300,000 (1.4 per cent of the total number of employees) and there was a shift of labour from the main export industries to the consumer goods and distributive industries. There were few major industrial disputes. One was in October, when oil-tanker drivers

Women at work in the workroom of the Castle Embroidery Company, Nottingham, 1953.

went on strike: the government called in the troops and it was all over within a week. In December more than 1 million engineering and shipbuilding workers went on a 24-hour strike in protest at the rejection of their claim for a 15 per cent wage increase.

Two months after the budget, a committee set up by the Ministry of Labour to advise on the employment of older persons issued its first report. This noted the rising number of people of retirement age – both men (who retired at 65) and women (60) – in the population and urged greater use of them and older workers generally. In particular it urged employers to dismantle any barriers limiting the promotion prospects of the older age group.

FOREIGN POLICY ISSUES

As a world power, Britain's expenditure on the armed services was high because of the country's continuing participation in the Korean War, its presence in the Suez Canal Zone in Egypt and maintenance of what was still an extensive British Empire. In 1953 this meant in particular significant military involvement in Kenya and Malaya as a result of the troubles which British rule now faced there.

Egypt

The British military presence in Egypt began in 1882. Although Britain had recognised Egypt's sovereign independence in 1922, the troops remained. In 1936 an Anglo-Egyptian treaty provided for the gradual withdrawal of the troops except from the canal zone, which was to remain under British protection. This was because of financial interests and the importance of the Suez Canal as a waterway. The British departure was postponed by the Italian invasion of Egypt in 1940 and the troops were to remain continuously on Egyptian soil until 1956. In October 1951, however, the Egyptians uni-laterally renounced the 1936 agreement.

These policy changes encouraged violence in the canal zone early in 1952 and King Farouk dismissed his Prime Minister Nahas Pasha for failing to maintain order. A series of administrations was

Two ships of the desert side by side.

The aftermath of the Suez negotiations. (© *Luton Museum Service*)

formed over the next few months but there was growing unrest in the country and the king continued to lose support. A *coup d'état* occurred on the night of 23 July under the direction of Major-General Mohammed Neguib, a popular figure with the military. A few days later King Farouk abdicated and his son Ahmed Fuad (born earlier that year) was proclaimed in his stead. Towards the end of the year the Egyptian cabinet issued a decree conferring supreme powers on General Neguib for six months, backdated to the time of the *coup*. The 1923 constitution was abolished in December and Egypt became a republic in June 1953.

Britain recognised Egypt as a republic within days of its declaration. But no agreement was reached on the question of British troops in the Suez Canal Zone after conversations between General Sir Brian Robertson and members of the Egyptian government in September. Negotiations had been adjourned indefinitely in May after several meetings and a number of incidents in the zone. Unless their presence was absolutely necessary, members of the British community in Egypt were advised to leave the country and for a while controls were imposed on traffic in and out of Ismailya. Churchill's first cabinet meeting after his illness (8 September) concerned possible Egyptian action against the British forces on the Suez Canal. There was talk of a military response but he urged caution, noting that Britain could block Egypt's sterling balances and thereby 'control the flow of oil to Cairo'.

Russian leaders flank the open coffin of Marshal Stalin in Moscow. From left to right: Molotov, Marshal Voroshilov, Beria, Premier Malenkov, Marshal Bulganin, Khruschev, Kaganovitch and Mikoyan, 12 March 1953.

Bermuda Conference

Churchill began the year in the USA with informal discussions with President-Elect Eisenhower; Eden and Butler visited Washington in March. Discussions centred around Europe, the Middle East and the Far East. The death of Stalin that month and the subsequent more friendly attitude adopted by his successor Malenkov towards the non-communist world led Churchill to urge a conference 'on the highest level' between the leading powers with a view to securing and safeguarding world peace. On 21 June it was announced that a conference had been arranged in Bermuda for 8 July. But Churchill's stroke of 23 June meant that the meeting was postponed until December. Churchill later saw this as a turning point, believing that if the conference had taken place in the summer he might have been able to persuade Eisenhower that a meeting with Malenkov would be useful.

Just before the Bermuda meeting took place, the Soviet Union proposed a four-power conference at foreign-secretary level in Berlin. This development gave an impetus to the December gathering of Eisenhower, Churchill and the French Prime Minister Laniel. Agreement on the Allied reply to the Soviet invitation was the first priority. Among the items Churchill also raised were matters of East–West relations, Germany and the European Defence Community. Churchill had little encouragement from either the French or the Americans for his proposed top-level talks with the Soviet Union, reluctantly complying with the joint reply to talks in Berlin which would take place in early 1954. Churchill was disappointed by the American response and that the conference, which he thought could do so much for international relations, achieved so little. This was his greatest disappointment since the war.

REFORM OF THE NATIONAL HEALTH SERVICE

The National Health Service (NHS) had been established by the Labour government in 1948. The first full year of the successor Conservative government, 1952/53, had seen a 7 per cent increase in expenditure; that for 1953/54 rose by only one-third of 1 per cent. This nominal rise was possible because economies had been achieved through staff reorganisation and area pooling of activities. Nevertheless the government (especially the Treasury) remained anxious over the NHS's mounting cost and in 1953 set up a committee to review current and prospective costs as well as to recommend how the money allocated could best be spent. Claude Guillebaud, who had been tutor to Iain Macleod (Minister of Health) while he was studying at Cambridge, was its chairman.

The committee reported in 1956 and concluded that the NHS provided good value for money and was indeed under-resourced as a percentage of rising national wealth. It urged greater capital expenditure, especially on hospitals, which were still suffering the ravages of the blitz; the abandoning of existing charges rather than the introduction of new ones such as a hospital boarding charge; and keeping eye and dental treatment within the NHS. The government's deputy chief medical officer later concluded that the appointment of Guillebaud and his recommendations probably saved the National Health Service.

Nye Bevan (centre), architect of the National Health Service, oversees plans of Woodberry Down Health Centre, the first in the country to have under one roof ante- and post-natal clinics, a child welfare centre and a school treatment centre. Bevan's Conservative successor continued support for the health service.

Winson Green Mental Hospital, Birmingham. Typical of scores of other mental hospitals, Winson Green was built in 1847 and designed to hold 800 patients: at the time of this photograph, 17 October 1953, there were 1,200. Overcrowding made it impossible to separate the curable from the incurable, and for some bedtime meant a mattress on the floor in a room used for other purposes during the day.

Early in 1953 Iain Macleod made a major speech recalling with pride the high level of public interest and involvement in local (often known as 'voluntary') hospitals before the Second World War. He now hoped that NHS hospitals could also enjoy such support and called for a return of the voluntary spirit to the new system. There was a positive and widespread response. Many hospitals set up volunteer groups or leagues of friends, who met on the premises. Such activities were previously believed to be unwelcome or not allowed.

The importance of management in the expanding NHS continued to be recognised. King Edward's Hospital Fund pioneered a year-long training course in London which began in September for those nurses likely to become matrons. The course emphasised the human dimension of management and the needs of patients. It arranged work experience in hotels and other organisations where personnel work was highly regarded.

LAW AND ORDER

Although the offence was committed and the judgment given in 1952, the consequences of the Craig/Bentley murder trial continued to be a major issue as 1953 opened. In the previous November Derek Bentley (aged nineteen) and Christopher Craig (aged sixteen) had set out to burgle a warehouse in West Croydon, Surrey. They were disturbed by the police and after what was viewed as incitement by Bentley ('Let him have it, Chris!'), Craig shot and killed a policeman. The jury found both Bentley and Craig guilty of the murder but recommended that mercy be shown to Bentley; Craig was too young to be hanged. The presiding judge, Lord Chief Justice Goddard, sentenced Bentley to death. The Home Secretary, Maxwell Fyfe ('the nearest thing to death in life', according to a contemporary Bar jingle), refused to grant a reprieve and ignored the considerable opposition which this case aroused. Bentley was hanged on 28 January. A few weeks earlier Detective Sergeant Fairfax had been awarded the George Cross for the bravery shown in the arrest of the two culprits.

The Rise in Youth Crime and the Response

Total indictable offences known to the police in 1953 had nearly doubled compared with those of the late 1930s; sexual offences had more than doubled and crimes of violence tripled. The Craig/Bentley trial epitomised and confirmed the anxiety over the rise in crime, especially that committed by the young, above all by boys, who committed ten times as many crimes as girls. There was, however, a recent growth in offences committed by young girls and great concern was expressed over the rise in those charged with promiscuous behaviour. Various explanations were offered for this and growing youth crime generally – the effects of the Second World War on the breakdown of home and family life as well as the growing disrespect for law because of the black market and its contentious hero, the spiv.

The government looked to schools – especially primary schools – to improve the behaviour of the young. It also passed the Prevention of Crime Act, which prohibited the carrying of any offensive weapon in public without lawful authority or reasonable excuse. This was seen as a new departure in law, being designed to *prevent* crimes of violence and specifically had the 'cosh boys' in mind.

Those who nevertheless went on to commit offences could now be dealt with in a variety of ways. Following the Criminal Justice Act (1948), prison was the last resort for those under twenty-one. Alternatives in 1953 included the remand home, which offered safe custody for boys and girls before or during appearance at court. It was in effect a short-term punitive detention centre. There was also Borstal and Approved School. The former took its name from a place in Kent where the first such institution was set up at the beginning of the century. There were over 100 Approved Schools in England

and Wales. They provided education and training for young offenders and children.

Finally, in 1953 there were three Attendance Centres and one Detention Centre, which was at Kidlington, Oxfordshire, and had been opened in August 1952. It was designed to accommodate fifty-five inmates aged between fourteen and seventeen. It was full by March. By this time a second such centre was being built at Goudhurst, Kent, for seventeen- to 21-year-olds. Youths were usually sentenced to Detention Centres for three months. The aim, in the language of the time, was to give them a 'short, sharp shock' to make it clear that the law could not be defied with impunity. Those sentenced to Attendance Centres were only required to be present for two to three hours on Saturday afternoons for upwards of twelve months. They would be provided with a suitable occupation and be taught how to make proper use of their leisure.

Moral Crime

Suicide, abortion and homosexuality (even in private between consenting adults) were all illegal in 1953. An active (or even suspected) homosexual frequently faced violence or blackmail and loss of employment. The number of people prosecuted for homosexual offences rose in the early 1950s primarily because of the increased political determination to bring such men to trial. In October 1952 the Home Secretary told the House of Commons that homosexuals were exhibitionists, proselytisers and a danger to others, especially the young. Such comments resulted in increased police action against homosexuals, especially if they were in the public eye.

The year saw the resignation of Ian Harvey, a Foreign Office minister, after being fined £5 for standing under a tree in St James's Park, London, 'misbehaving with a guardsman', and the conviction of John Gielgud, recently knighted in the coronation honours, for an indecency offence. Some in the press called for the honour to be withdrawn. On his first appearance on stage after the conviction, Gielgud was given an ovation.

Art, Protest and Wilful Damage

In 1952 there was an international competition for a monument to the Unknown Political Prisoner. People from over fifty countries entered the competition. The British sculptor Reg Butler won the prize (£4,500), even though he was up against people like Gabo and Hepworth, who each received £750. The model, along with other entries, was first displayed in the Tate Gallery, London, on 14 March 1953. The model

Sir John Gielgud.

was fourteen inches high and described by *The Times* as 'like an iron cage on a stick'. The following day it was deliberately destroyed by Laszlo Szilvassy, a stateless person of Hungarian origin. After bending the wire and throwing it on to the ground, he handed a note to the attendant explaining his actions. He argued that reducing the memory of the dead and the suffering of the living to scrap metal was just as much a crime as to reduce them to ashes. Szilvassy appeared before Bow Street Magistrates Court and asked to be tried by jury. He was remanded in custody until mid-April and then pleaded guilty. He was conditionally discharged and ordered to pay 10 guineas costs.

Butler was able to produce another model and hoped that it would achieve the height and fame of Nelson's Column. The sculpture alluded to the symbols of how people had suffered for their beliefs – the cage, cross, guillotine, scaffold and watch-tower would all have featured. Cold War politics meant that it was never constructed.

The Christie Murders and Trial

On 24 March 1953 the new tenant of a ground-floor flat at 10 Rillington Place, Notting Hill, London, found three concealed bodies in the kitchen. Police then found the body of Mrs Ethel Christie, wife of the former tenant, under the floorboards of the front room and the remains of two more women in the garden. The search began for John Christie, who had disappeared a few days earlier. On 31 March PC Thomas Ledger saw Christie on Putney Bridge and arrested him. The trial of Christie for the murder of his wife began on 22 June in No. 1 Court at the Old Bailey.

During Christie's fifteen-year tenancy of the flat several murders had been committed in the property. These included in 1950 Mrs Beryl Evans, who occupied the top-floor flat of the same house, and was now found strangled with her baby daughter Geraldine in the outhouse laundry room behind Christie's flat. Her husband Timothy had been convicted of their murders after making an unprompted confession to having disposed of Mrs Evans's body down the drain outside the house.

During interrogation, Christie confessed to some murders and, when on trial, to having killed Beryl Evans, but he denied killing Geraldine. He later withdrew this latter denial, claiming that he believed the greater the number of murders he was supposed to have committed the better his chance of being declared insane. The jury, out for 85 minutes, found Christie guilty of the murder of his wife and three other women. He was sentenced to death and hanged in Pentonville Prison, London, by Albert Pierrepoint, who had also been responsible for the execution of Timothy Evans.

The Christie case: 10 Rillington Place, Notting Hill, London, and the women who were murdered.

Given anxiety over whether Evans had been innocent, the Home Secretary initiated a private inquiry which was carried out by Mr John Scott Henderson. He concluded that Evans had indeed killed his wife and child. These findings were reported to Parliament in 1953 but a *public* inquiry was denied. That had to wait until the winter of 1965/66 and was held in the wake of *10 Rillington Place*, Sir Ludovic Kennedy's 1961 account of the two cases. Mr Justice Brabin concluded that it was 'more probable than not' that Evans had killed his wife but did not kill his daughter. As Evans had been hanged for murdering Geraldine he was given a posthumous pardon. His remains were exhumed from Pentonville prison and buried elsewhere.

The Christie case resumed: being remanded for a week, John Reginald Halliday Christie, aged 55, made a further appearance at Clerkenwell Magistrates Court, charged with the murders of four women, his wife, Ethel Christie (aged 54); Rita Elizabeth Nelson (aged 24); Kathleen Maloney (aged 26); and Hectorina McKay Maclennan (aged 25). The bodies were among those found in the house and garden at 10 Rillington Place. This photograph shows how numerous women were in the crowd waiting outside the courts.

Government Report on Capital Punishment

On 23 September the Royal Commission on Capital Punishment, chaired by Sir Ernest Gowers, reported. Its primary remit had been to consider limitations on and modifications to those offences which carried the death penalty. It recommended raising the minimum age for execution from eighteen to twenty-one, and that suicide should remain illegal but any survivor of a suicide pact, while still to be regarded as guilty of murder, should not suffer the death penalty but instead be imprisoned for life unless the person concerned had killed the other party. Unlike the American system, the Royal Commission could not accept that there were divisions (or 'degrees') of murder, nor that judges should be able to decide whether a life sentence could be substituted for the death penalty. There was to be no parliamentary discussion of the Report until 1955.

'On Top of the World': The Conquest of Everest

'THE ABODE OF SNOW'

Himalaya is the name given to the vast mountain system in central Asia lying along the south edge of the plateau of Tibet and enclosed by the Rivers Indus and Brahmaputra. It extends in an immense curve about 1,500 miles in the east from the Karakoram range through Pakistan, India, Tibet, Nepal, Sikkim and Bhutan. It is between 100 and 150 miles wide. Of the thirteen mountains in the world which exceed 25,000 feet, eight are in Nepal. The range's name is a Sanskrit word and translates as 'the abode of snow': all the high peaks are permanently snow-capped, the snowline varying between 15,000 and 19,000 feet.

There is a northern range and a southern range. The latter is divided into three – the Outer, the Lesser and the Great Himalayas, the last of which is the main range. The mountains on the Great Himalayas have an average height of about 20,000 feet and contain the highest peaks, including Nanga Parbat (26,660 feet), Kanchenjunga (28,165 feet) and, the highest in the world, Everest (29,028 feet). This mountain is in the north-eastern corner of Nepal, on the border with Tibet and partly hidden by neighbouring peaks. Resembling a pyramid, Mount Everest has three wide faces and three great ridges – the North-East, West and South-East. The frontier between Nepal and Tibet crosses the mountain by the West and South-East Ridges.

Everest could and still can best be climbed during the pre-monsoon season. Conditions are at their best then, with snow cover at its firmest and the weather gradually becoming warmer, especially between mid-May and mid-June. After several previous attempts the conquest of Mount Everest was finally achieved on Friday 29 May 1953.

PEAK XV – ITS HEIGHT AND NAME

Until the middle of the nineteenth century, Kanchenjunga (28,165 feet), a peak to the east of Everest and on the Sikkim border, was regarded as the highest mountain in the world. In 1849, however, the British began the Great Trigonometrical Survey of India, using an idea devised by Sir George Everest, the British Surveyor-General of India between 1830 and 1843. The survey involved a series of measurements (or triangulations) of India itself but included the mountains of independent Nepal. The surveyors were denied access to Nepal itself and could only make rather incomplete observations from the plains and foothills of India. Few of the mountains in Nepal were known by name to the surveyors, so they were all given Roman numerals. Everest was Peak XV. Six observation stations had been used for the sightings of this peak; the average distance over which the readings were taken was 111 miles. In 1852 the height of this peak was calculated to be 29,002 feet, making it the highest known mountain in the world. This was still its presumed height in 1953; only subsequently was this increased by 26 feet to the tentative current calculation of 29,028 feet.

Peak XV was renamed at the suggestion of Everest's successor as Surveyor-General of India, Sir Andrew Waugh, but not without opposition. In 1857, when the idea was discussed at the Royal Geographical Society in London, Sir George made clear his objections to such a proposal: people indigenous to the area could neither write nor pronounce his name. He was also aware that to give his name to an Asian mountain could create an unwelcome precedent. The official policy was that mountains should be known by their local name. Such a view was supported by geographical bodies throughout the world.

Various local names were already known to the Royal Geographical Society and it provisionally adopted the Nepalese name Gaurisankar in 1862, only changing it to Mount Everest three years later. In 1903, however, Captain Henry Wood, under the instructions of Lord Curzon, then Viceroy of India, went into Nepal and concluded that Everest and Gaurisankar were two *different* peaks. It was now argued that there was no indigenous name for the world's highest mountain. But this was not so: the Tibetan name 'Chomolungma' or some similarly spelt name in western script had been known since the early eighteenth century. It could be translated as 'Goddess Mother of the World' and was a more appropriate and respectful name. Significantly, when, during the Everest reconnaissance expedition of 1921 George Mallory sought to give English names to various peaks, he was overruled and Tibetan names were used instead. As the 50th anniversary of the 1953 conquest approached there was renewed pressure for worldwide adoption of a local name for this most celebrated site.

Sir George Everest, the military engineer who conducted a survey of India from 1818 to 1843. He was appointed Superintendent of the Great Trigonometrical Survey of India in 1823 and Surveyor-General of India in 1830. In 1852 he measured the height of Peak XV in the Himalayas as 29,002 feet above sea level. In 1865, in honour of his work as a surveyor, Peak XV was renamed Mount Everest.

Sketch of Andrew Irvine by Francis Helps. (© *John Noel Photographic Collection*)

ATTEMPTS ON MOUNT EVEREST BEFORE 1953

The British expedition which succeeded in climbing Everest in 1953 was the eighth to make the attempt. There had also been three reconnaissance expeditions – in 1921, 1935 and 1951 – as well as a foray in 1913. In that year Captain John Noel had entered Tibet illegally and, after darkening his hair and skin, disguised himself as a follower of Islam. He came within forty miles of Everest before being turned back by Tibetan soldiers. This was the closest any westerner had yet been to the mountain. In March 1919 the now Major Noel gave a well-attended lecture to the Royal Geographical Society entitled 'A journey to Tashirak in southern Tibet and the eastern approaches to Mount Everest'. The enthusiasm aroused at the meeting and in the media led to renewed interest in the mountain.

Consequently it was in 1920, when relations with the Tibetan government were friendly, that permission was first given for a party under Colonel Howard-Bury to explore the whole range and find a route up Mount Everest. During the summer of 1921 the northern approaches to the mountain were explored. The party ascended the main or west Rongbuk glacier, missing the narrower opening of the eastern branch and with it their only possible line to the summit. From Karta Shekar, however, the party discovered a pass up Lhakpa La (22,000 feet) leading to the head of the Rongbuk glacier. The saddle north of Everest was climbed on 24 September by, among others, George Mallory, and named North Col (a col is a dip in a ridge, usually between two peaks) or Chang La.

In May the following year Brigadier-General Bruce led a second expedition. It reached 27,300 feet but the monsoon snow prevented any further progress. The first fatalities ever recorded on Everest occurred at this time, when seven Sherpas from India died in an avalanche. General Bruce led another expedition in 1924. Because of snow, the camp on North Col was not established until May. The party was then forced to descend and Bruce had to return as a result of contracting malaria. The group, now led by Norton, resumed the climb. In early June George Mallory and Andrew Irvine headed for the summit. As they climbed up the north-east ridge a heavy mist rolled in. When it lifted, no trace of the climbers could be found, and Mallory's body was not discovered until 1999. It is not known whether they reached the summit.

Further, failed, attempts followed in the 1930s, including the tragic death of Maurice Wilson on what proved to be a futile attempt in 1934 to climb the mountain accompanied by only three Sherpas. After the Second World War it was again impossible for political

Sketch of George Mallory by Francis Helps. (© *John Noel Photographic Collection*)

reasons to approach Everest through Tibet. In 1951, however, the Nepalese government gave permission for a reconnaissance of the mountain from its southern side. The resultant British expedition climbed the Khumbu Icefall which Mallory had seen from the west and traced a possible line up the Western Cwm to the South Col, the high saddle between Lhotse and Everest. There were two Swiss expeditions in 1952. Both reached the South Col and opened up the main route up the face. However, bad weather prevented them from going much further. It was likely that 1953 would finally witness the ascent of Mount Everest.

Members of the earlier expedition. Back row, left to right: Andrew Irvine, George Mallory, Edward Norton, Noel Odell, John Macdonald. Front row: Edward Shebbeare, Geoffrey Bruce, Howard Somervell, Bentley Beetham. (© *John Noel Photographic Collection*)

THE 1953 BRITISH EXPEDITION TEAM

The team was led by Colonel Hunt; its deputy was Dr Evans. There were twelve other members of the expedition including a physiologist employed by the Medical Research Council, a cameraman with Countryman Films Limited (the cost of whose contract helped finance the team) and a correspondent for *The Times*, which had bought exclusive newspaper rights. The head Sherpa, known as the sirdar, was Tenzing Norgay.

HUNT THE LEADER

The two main organisations behind mountaineering in Britain were the Royal Geographical Society and the Alpine Club. In 1947 they had established an informal joint Himalayan Committee to consider once more the conquest of Everest. Eric Shipton, who had been to Everest five times and had led the 1951 expedition, was appointed leader of the 1952 training expedition as only the Swiss had been granted permission to attempt the climb that year. Britain's turn would come again in 1953, and Shipton expected to lead that. However, the Committee – especially its chairman, Claude Elliot – had other ideas. It feared further disappointment under Shipton's rather lacklustre leadership. Fail now, he argued, and Britain would not have another opportunity until 1956, by which time it was likely that another nation would have been the first to reach the summit. Succeed in coronation year and a new Elizabethan age would truly have dawned.

COLONEL JOHN HUNT

Henry Cecil John Hunt was born in Simla, India, in June 1910. His father was an army officer and a mountaineer who died in action in 1914. John Hunt followed and excelled in both his father's careers. He was educated at Marlborough College, Wiltshire, and then Sandhurst Military Academy, where he headed the list for his year. He was commissioned in the King's Royal Rifle Corps in 1930.

He began climbing in the Alps when he was fifteen years old and rock climbing in Britain at about the same time. He gained further experience of climbing while serving in the political intelligence division of the Indian police during the 1930s. Only ill-health prevented him from joining the 1936 British expedition to Everest. He served in Italy and Egypt during the Second World War. In 1940 his responsibilities included being Chief Instructor of the Commando Mountain and Snow Warfare school. He resumed climbing after the Second World War. By 1952 he had been a member of five Himalayan expeditions.

EDMUND HILLARY

Edmund Hillary was born in 1919 in Auckland, New Zealand, and educated there. He became a bee-keeper (his father's business) when he was seventeen and took particular delight in this occupation. But he had other outdoor interests as well. He played a major role in developing winter ski-mountaineering in that country. During the Second World War he was a navigator in the Royal New Zealand Air Force. He began mountaineering in New Zealand.

TENZING NORGAY

Tenzing, originally known as Namgyal Wangdi, was born in eastern Nepal in 1914. He was one of thirteen children. A devout Buddhist, he was renamed Tenzing Norgay following a visit as a child to a lama who informed him that he, Tenzing, was the reincarnation of a wealthy man who had died recently. The lama suggested the new name, which could be translated as 'Wealthy-Fortunate-Follower-of-Religion'. His subsequent life displayed all these qualities.

Ever since childhood Tenzing had been eager to be a mountaineer, and in 1935 went as a porter with the Everest reconnaissance expedition of that year. Determined to reach the summit of the mountain he knew as Chomolungma, he took part in more expeditions than any other climber. During the Second World War he served as a guide with the Chitral scouts and as an Indian army ski instructor. Following further mountaineering experience in the postwar period, he went on the Swiss expedition to Everest in 1952 and was chosen later that year by Colonel Hunt to be sirdar of the Sherpas and climber in his 1953 expedition.

Colonel Hunt was known to the Joint Himalayan Committee through his friendship with its secretary, Basil Goodfellow. He considered Hunt to be a 'terrific thruster' and was determined to have him as leader if only for the final assault. The chairman supported Hunt's inclusion, envisaging him as assault though not expedition leader.

Misunderstandings as to the intended role of Hunt on the expedition led to an unsatisfactory meeting between him and

A clear view of Everest.
(© *John Noel Photographic Collection*)

Eric Shipton, who expected to head the 1953 British Everest expedition but was replaced by John Hunt.

Shipton. Both Elliot and Goodfellow, however, were determined that Hunt should hold a senior position and he was made co-leader with special responsibility for organisation in London and the final assault on the peak. Shipton would not accept this and offered his resignation, which the committee accepted.

On 11 September 1952 the Himalayan Committee formally asked Colonel John Hunt to lead the British expedition to Everest in the following spring. Existing members of the expedition, including Edmund Hillary, were horrified at the outcome and initially one member intended to withdraw. Shipton persuaded him to remain with the expedition and, although he himself refused to serve under Hunt, assisted in the planning stages. However, Hunt proved, as expected, to be a brilliant organiser and determined leader, recognising the wider issues at stake.

CHOOSING THE TEAM

Hunt took up his duties officially on 9 October 1952 and within the month had produced the basic programme for the expedition. He believed a team of ten climbers plus Sherpas would be sufficient. A selection committee of Hunt, Goodfellow and Shipton was formed. Hunt restricted membership to men from Britain and the Commonwealth, although before Hunt became involved American participation had been invited. Reluctantly Hunt agreed to three non-climbers accompanying the expedition: a physiologist (Griff Pugh), a cameraman (Tom Stobart) with Countryman Films Limited and a journalist from *The Times* (James, later Jan, Morris). *The Times* had a well-established history of carrying reports on mountaineering and had covered pre-war expeditions to Everest. Morris's reports released Hunt of some of the burden of writing despatches.

Many applications to join the team were received, including one from a member of the 1924 expedition. Now aged sixty-six, he was rejected, as was Chris Brasher, a future Olympic Gold Medallist. There were to be three attempts on the summit on three successive days. Should they all fail there would be a second expedition in the autumn.

INITIAL PREPARATIONS

Hunt placed considerable emphasis on the nature and quality of the equipment to be used. Every climber was provided with shell clothing consisting of anorak and overtrousers of a close-woven material made of cotton warp and nylon weft. It weighed only 4.75

ounces per square yard and was totally impervious to winds up to 100 mph. The garments were also showerproof. The tents were of the same material. That for the final assault could accommodate two and, together with the groundsheet, weighed four pounds. The boots used at this stage were designed by the British Boot, Shoe and Allied Trades Research Association in Kettering. They were two and a quarter pounds lighter than those used on previous expeditions: there were no nails and the soles were made of lightweight artificial rubber. Great attention was also paid to oxygen. The climbers responsible for such equipment were scientists, and the main contractors (Normalair) and the Ministry of Supply did not charge. Similarly the Swiss gave details of the oxygen which their expedition had left on the mountain in 1952 and appropriate adapters were taken by the climbers. Such supplies were crucial not only for climbing at the high altitudes involved but also, and this was new for 1953, for getting to sleep.

THE ROUTE TO THE TOP

The main party sailed from Tilbury for Bombay in the SS *Stratheden* on 12 February. Some of the others, including Hunt and Deputy Leader Evans, flew to Kathmandu soon afterwards. The two New Zealanders, Hillary and Lowe, arrived there the following month, as did the twenty Sherpas with their sirdar Tenzing Norgay whom Hunt had specifically invited to take on this responsibility. Everyone

Everest conqueror: this picture, made by a British Movietone News cameraman who went out to meet the returning victorious British Everest Expedition, shows Hillary having a cup of tea with Tenzing Norgay.

had left the city by mid-March and soon began a period of training and acclimatisation near Mount Everest.

By 24 April it was possible to start ferrying supplies to the head of the Western Cwm. Two forms of oxygen apparatus, the closed- and the open-circuit types, were to be used. With open-circuit apparatus, the climber breathes partly from the outside air. Hunt decided that team members Bourdillon and Evans, who were both familiar with the closed circuit, should make the first attempt from the South Col. Hillary and Tenzing were to follow, using open-circuit equipment and from a higher camp. Bourdillon and Evans reached the south summit of Everest on 26 May but were too late in the day and too tired to go further. There were also problems with the oxygen equipment. The first of the three attempts had failed.

THE FINAL PHASE

Early on the morning of 28 May Hillary and Tenzing set off. They were preceded by three others who carried supplies to 27,900 feet and Ridge Camp (Camp XI) was established. It was from there the following day that Hillary and Tenzing were to attempt the last 1,100 feet or so to the summit. The wind dropped and the next morning dawned sunny and calm. At 6.30 a.m., after a breakfast of sardines on biscuits and sweet hot lemon water, Hillary and Tenzing set off. Their protection included wearing three pairs of gloves of silk, woollen and windproof material. By 9 a.m. the two men were on the south summit with only a few hundred feet left to climb, albeit the steepest yet encountered.

Hillary worked out a route, and he and Tenzing took it in turns to cut steps in the ice, a crucial but physically exhausting activity. On one occasion ice blocked the rubber exhaust tube of Tenzing's oxygen source but Hillary cleared it before Tenzing passed out. On they went until they found their way blocked by a rock cliff some forty feet high according to Hillary; fifteen feet according to Tenzing. It had no climbing holds and would have to be skirted round. Taking the west side would have involved *descending* some hundred feet – but they were just too tired for the additional effort involved. The east route was a vertical split between the cliff and a cornice leaning over the valley. The cornice was already beginning to break away from the cliff and could crash at any time 10,000 feet into the valley below. But there was no alternative. Slowly, Hillary leading, they made their way to the top of the split, yet still the summit was hidden by innumerable ice-humps and the path was apparently endless. But then it began to slope away. They had made it; they were on the summit of Mount Everest.

LIFE AT THE TOP

Tenzing Norgay with an array
of oxygen bottles at his feet.

On their arrival at 11.30 a.m., like other climbers on reaching a mountain's summit, they shook hands, Tenzing waved his arms in the air and both thumped each other on the back until, despite the oxygen, they were breathless. The relief was very real as physiologists had warned that the summit of Everest was a very marginal altitude and might be extremely dangerous. For a brief while, however, they turned off their oxygen supplies and removed their masks.

Hillary took out his camera which he had carried under his clothing to prevent it from freezing. Tenzing unwound four flags from around his axe. They were tied together on a string, which was fastened to the blade of the axe. Hillary photographed Tenzing

Khatmandu, Nepal, 1 July 1953: Edmund Hillary relaxing at the base of Mount Everest.

holding up the axe. The order of the flags from top to bottom was that of the United Nations, the UK, Nepal and India. Afterwards, as he required the axe for his descent, Tenzing untied the string that held the flags and spread them across the summit. He buried the ends of the string deep in the snow.

Tenzing had never used a camera and the summit of Everest was not thought the best place to teach him. Consequently Hillary alone continued photographing everything around him and looked for, but failed to find, any evidence that Mallory had reached the summit in 1924. Tenzing meanwhile made a shallow hole in the snow. In it he buried a coloured pencil which his young daughter Nima had given him, biscuits, chocolate and a packet of sweets, small gifts to the gods of Chomolungma whom he believed inhabited the summit. Hillary passed him a small cloth cat to bury which Hunt had given him as a mascot. Hillary dug alongside Tenzing and buried, as requested, a white crucifix which Hunt had also given him. Then, having made some seats of snow, they ate a bar of mintcake.

THE FIRST DESCENT FROM EVEREST

Hillary and Tenzing remained at the summit for about fifteen minutes before making their way back. Feeling a great closeness to the divine there, Tenzing gave thanks for their success and prayed for a safe return. Both men were eager to return to the south summit, being mindful of their consumption of oxygen (even at a reduced level they now had only about four and half hours' supply) and of the increased dangers brought on by climbing when tired, especially when heavily loaded. They were thirsty too, and there was little liquid available; eating snow would only have made things worse. Tenzing shared his water bottle with Hillary. In it was a concoction of water, sugar, lemon crystals and raspberry jam.

At about two in the afternoon, however, they reached their tent and Tenzing heated some sweet lemon juice. A little later they were met on the slopes above the South Col by fellow New Zealander George Lowe and rewarded with more hot drinks. They had just enough oxygen to make it to the next camp. Another climber there, Noyce, explained to Hillary that Hunt had requested that, should the climb prove successful, two sleeping bags in the form of the letter 'T'(meaning Top) were to be laid on a snow slope on the edge of South Col so that it might be seen from Camp IV. Strong winds meant that, much to the puzzlement of others who were unaware of the code, Noyce and a Sherpa had to lie on them in the bitter cold for about ten minutes. Unfortunately, despite these efforts, their signal was not seen – either because of cloud or because no one was looking in that direction at the time.

The journey from there involved stops at the various camps which had been set up en route. At the Advance Base Camp they met Hunt, who delighted in their success. The expedition rum was consumed and the patron of the expedition, the Duke of Edinburgh, was toasted. They also drank to Eric Shipton, acknowledging his contribution to the success.

By 2 June, Coronation Day, the whole expedition was reassembled at the base camp, which had a radio. Hillary tuned into the BBC in London and heard the announcement concerning the expedition's success. It transformed his initial sense of satisfaction in reaching the summit to one now of excitement at what had indeed been achieved. Hunt was surprised that the expedition's success was known before Coronation Day. He had hoped that this might happen but, given the delayed start and the failure of the first assault, was resigned to the news following rather than preceding the great event. On Coronation Day, because of limited space, members sat on the ground or on ration boxes to drink the loyal toast.

A couple of days later Hunt visited the monks at the nearby Thyangboche camp, informed them of the expedition's success and made a donation for the repair of the monastery's roof. The lamas there had already planned to break years of quiet meditation and hold a lavish party. The abbot, although welcoming, remained un-convinced about their achievement, merely congratulating them on 'nearly reaching the summit of Chomolungma'.

INFORMING THE REST OF THE WORLD AND ITS REACTION

Interest in the British expedition was worldwide. But *The Times* had exclusive rights and planned accordingly. The original intention was for James Morris, its correspondent and a member of the expedition, to send a message in code and by runner to the British Ambassador in Kathmandu. There it would be transmitted by radio to London and be in the newspapers around eight days after the news had first reached base camp. Morris realised while on Everest that there was a quicker way – by using a runner to Namche Bazar and then by transmitting the news by radio from there to Kathmandu. Following a first, false, report of failure by India Wireless News, the true state of affairs was sent by Morris in the code which he had devised. It read 'snow conditions bad stop advanced base abandoned yesterday stop awaiting improvement'. This translated as 'Summit of Everest reached on May 29 by Hillary and Tenzing'. Morris also had coded catastrophe messages and prepared obituaries.

The British Ambassador who forwarded the message to London did not inform anyone else for more than a day. The idea was for Queen Elizabeth II to have the news first. However, this strategy meant that those in the region concerned did not receive the news until 2 June, when All India Radio carried news of the success which it had received from the *other* side of the world. This was true even for the King of Nepal, whose kingdom was the home of Mount Everest. Nevertheless he subsequently hosted a grand reception for the team. The King awarded Tenzing the Nepal Tara or Star of Nepal, the highest decoration not reserved for royalty; the Prime Minister bestowed on Hillary and Hunt the Gorkha Dakshina Bahu or the Order of the Gurkha Right Hand, which was a lesser award.

The Queen and Churchill sent telegrams of congratulation to the expedition via the British Ambassador in Kathmandu. The news was announced over loudspeakers along the coronation route. Thereafter telegrams and soon letters poured in. Hunt sent cables of humble appreciation to the Queen and the Prime Minister. He also informed the Himalayan Committee that Hillary and Tenzing would now return with others to Britain.

WELCOME HOME

Members of the expedition, including Hunt, Hillary and Tenzing (with his family), arrived in Britain on 3 July. As Hunt disembarked from the BOAC

DAILY HERALD

WEDNESDAY June 3 1953

Call it Mount ELIZABETH!

SO the greatest adventure story of 1953 has the happiest possible ending.

Mount Everest, 29,002-foot highest point on earth, is climbed by members of a British expedition—and the news is learned on the historic eve of Queen Elizabeth's Coronation.

In the superb bravery, endurance and skill of Edmund Hillary, of New Zealand, and Sen Tensing, of India, is epitomised not only the effort of hundreds who contributed to their ascent, but the triumphant spirit of the whole Commonwealth in this splendid hour.

Such victory calls for permanent celebration. The *Daily Herald* has a suggestion to make.

WHY NOT A NEW NAME?

Mount Everest stands partly in Tibet and partly in Nepal. Thus it is nobody's particular national property. Its name in the surrounding lands is Chomolungma, which means Goddess Mother of the Snows.

It was called Everest by the British after Sir George Everest, Surveyor-General of India, when, in 1852, it was first discovered by triangulation to be the world's highest mountain.

Because of the happy timing of its conquest, it might with propriety be now renamed **MOUNT ELIZABETH.**

Those who conquer a great new peak in remote territory have long had the privilege of naming it, although the local name, if any, is usually retained.

But Everest already bears a British name—and of seven previous expeditions which attacked the summit, all were British except last year's two Swiss attempts.

THE BRITISH PIONEERS

Of three reconnaissances, involving exploration of hundreds of miles of unknown territory—and including that of 1951 which pioneered last week's route to the top—all were British.

No race has a better claim to write into the history books a wonderful success story under the chapter heading of— **MOUNT ELIZABETH.**

All the Western world, which has watched with sympathetic admiration both the Coronation and Col. Hunt's expedition, would surely applaud such a change.

Argonaut aeroplane at London he waved the Union Jack from his ice axe. The party was greeted by the Secretary of State for War, Brigadier Anthony Head, as the expedition's leader was a soldier. Some five hundred people were there to greet them and the newspapers and newsreels proclaimed 'Everest Heroes Home'. The diverse national backgrounds of the three leading figures were often portrayed as a living embodiment of the Commonwealth ideal, together with elements of British identity.

Hillary visited his sister in Norfolk while Hunt returned to his home at Llanfair Waterdine, a village on the Welsh border. Here he stood in a small cart, garlanded with flowers and waving the British flag from his ice axe as local farmers towed him up the hill to his home. The Welsh National Party, however, announced at a rally that Hunt had sent them a message and it was already known that he had flown the Welsh flag at his camps on Everest. The War Office reminded Hunt that his military position required him to remain non-partisan. Tenzing stayed in and toured London, giving interviews.

On 6 June it was announced that Hillary and Hunt would be honoured by the Queen; no announcement could be made regarding Tenzing because, not being a British subject, consultation with the Nepalese and Indian governments was required. On 16 July the climbers, together with 8,000 other people, attended the second Royal Garden Party of the year at Buckingham Palace. Amid the pouring rain the bands of the Life Guards and the Plymouth division of the Royal Marines played alternately. One of the works featured was Handel's 'Water Music'. The waitresses on duty in front of the tea pavilion wore transparent capes with hoods over their uniforms. Although always available in case of bad weather, this was only the second time since the war that they had been needed.

Colonel John Hunt waves the flag with Sherpa Tenzing on his left and Edmund Hillary on his right, having arrived at London Airport after their conquest of Mount Everest, July 1953.

Everest heroes Tenzing (left) and Hillary (right) after King Tribhuvana had conferred honours on them, 25 June 1953.

The Queen was sheltered by an umbrella held by the Lord Chamberlain; the guests whom she met were sheltered by ushers. Shortly afterwards the three key figures were admitted to a drawing room. Hillary and Hunt were knighted and Tenzing invested with the George Medal. Tenzing was not given a British knighthood because the Indian Prime Minister, Jawaharlal Nehru, refused to allow him to accept such a potent symbol of British authority in the days of the Raj. The honour granted was allowed, and the country later issued a stamp to commemorate the climb. The New Zealand Prime Minister, Sidney Holland, had accepted it on Hillary's behalf before the latter had been informed.

The Queen gave all the climbers coronation medals engraved with the words 'Mount Everest Expedition'. In the evening the Duke of Edinburgh presided at a small state dinner specifically for men only. A larger, mixed, reception followed at Lancaster House.

Britons conquer Everest—
AND THEY TOOK GRAPE-NUTS!

Great event of a great year! Everest is conquered at last—and by *British* climbers! For success in this hazardous adventure, every item of equipment, every ounce of food had to do its full share—and more. And the climbers on this triumphant British expedition chose Grape-Nuts to take with them.

WHY THEY CHOSE GRAPE-NUTS

Grape-Nuts are *concentrated* goodness. Look at that handy packet. Twelve full ounces, as much as the biggest cereal packet gives you. That's one reason why the Everest climbers took Grape-Nuts—less to carry.

The other reason is *energy*. Quick energy. Double-baking converts the starch in Grape-Nuts into dextrose—and your body turns dextrose into energy *fast*. And in the hustle of modern life, *you* need what Grape-Nuts can give you, too.

Try Grape-Nuts tomorrow. They're delicious, with a rich malty flavour all their own. Serve them for breakfast with milk and sugar, and your family, like the Everest climbers, will be on top of the world!

Grape-Nuts

ANOTHER FINE PRODUCT OF
ALFRED BIRD & SONS LTD, BIRMINGHAM 19

AFTERMATH

Hillary returned briefly to New Zealand in August. Here he was presented with an easy chair shaped like the top of Mount Everest. He returned a few weeks later accompanied by Miss Louise Rose, whom he married on 3 September. Hunt embarked on a lecture tour and wrote *The Ascent of Everest*, which appeared in December. By then he had been made a brigadier and assistant commandant at the military staff college in Camberley. Tenzing returned home.

A film entitled *The Conquest of Everest* opened in October to a royal première and was soon shown in cinemas throughout Britain. The film made much of the two concurrent crowning events of the year – Everest and the coronation. In it the photograph of Tenzing on the summit is followed by the relaying of

the news to those on the coronation route. Images of the Queen's carriage in London precede Tenzing and others riding in state in Kathmandu. All these aspects and more came together to portray what many called 'Coronation Everest'.

Sir Edmund Hillary and his bride, the former Miss Louise Rose, as they leave the chapel of the Diocesan High School Auckland College, following their marriage in September 1953.

FOUR

The Coronation: The Nation Prepares

DECIDING AND ANNOUNCING THE CORONATION DATE

King George VI died suddenly at Sandringham, early on the morning of Wednesday 6 February 1952. The (present) Queen Elizabeth was in Kenya at the time, the first sovereign since 1714 (George I) to accede to the British throne while abroad. The King was buried nine days later. Understandably the intervening days were mostly concerned with the immediate formalities of one monarch's demise and the accession of another. Yet within a week of the King's death – 11 February – the cabinet had its first discussions on the timing of the coronation. It was decided that it could not take place in 1952 as this would detract from the government's focus on strengthening the economy. A delay until the summer of 1953 was deemed more appropriate and might yield political advantage in the subsequent General Election thought likely to be held early in 1955 (as indeed it was). The Conservative gain in the Sunderland by-election in May 1953 was partly attributed to its association with the then imminent coronation.

Churchill, almost seventy-seven when he became Prime Minister in October 1951, had intimated at the time that he would resign after one year in office. But following King George's death he was now less eager to stand down. He continued to enjoy both the premiership and his relationship with the new monarch, perhaps seeing similarities with his predecessor Lord Melbourne and the young Queen Victoria. He would prolong his weekly audiences with the Queen, especially if the subject-matter extended beyond politics to such mutual interests as horse-racing and polo.

Charles Moran, Churchill's doctor, noted that the premier was determined that the coronation should take place before his retirement – and that he wanted to delay the ceremony for as long as possible. But other countries where the Queen was also head of state wanted her to visit them – notably Australia and New Zealand – but only after she had been crowned.

The Wakamba Dance, Kenya, in preparation for the coronation.

Some consideration was given to holding the coronation in late May 1953. But this was eventually rejected because the Whitsun Bank Holiday fell on the last Monday of that month. To hold it the day after would, the cabinet argued, cost too much in lost production. Therefore the following Tuesday (2 June) was chosen, in part also because Meteorological Office forecasts suggested that this was likely to be a particularly promising summer's day. Those wishing or needing to travel to London could do so on the Monday, which would both be easier and, not being a Sunday, less controversial. The Wednesday of that week was ruled out because it was Derby Day. The coronation date was formally announced on 28 April 1952 and the coronation proclamation issued at the four traditional sites in London (St James's Palace, Charing Cross, Temple Bar and the Royal Exchange) in early June. The year-long lead-up to the coronation was deliberate, as both the administrative and commercial preparations – notably the manufacture of souvenirs and street decorations – were extensive. The civil estimates for 1952 provided £360,000 for the event; a further £1,200,000 was required in 1953. Seat sales would generate some £648,000, but this still meant that the day would cost almost £1 million.

PREPARATIONS IN 1952

A Coronation Committee was created in April and chaired by the Duke of Edinburgh. It had thirty-six members including representatives from the UK, Canada, Australia, New Zealand, Pakistan and Ceylon. Members included the Archbishop of Canterbury (Dr Fisher), Winston Churchill, Clement Attlee, Lord Woolton and Earl Jowitt. The Committee's remit was quite wide, and various sub-committees were established following the first meeting in May, including one under the 16th Duke of Norfolk who, as hereditary Earl Marshal, had a key role in the preparations for the coronation. This position dated back to the reign of Richard III (1483), and conferred on the Duke an honorarium of £20 for fulfilling the role. Another major figure was David Eccles, who headed the Ministry of Works and was to be knighted the day after the coronation. He described himself as 'the Earl Marshal's handyman'. It was his task, he said, to arrange flowers, floodlighting, fireworks and, above all, to 'set the stage and build a theatre inside Westminster Abbey'.

The Coronation Throne with the Stone of Scone. (© PA Photos)

One crucial prop, however, was (back) in place – the Stone of Scone. On Christmas morning 1950, the stone had been removed from Westminster Abbey, its traditional resting-place at that time, by three Scottish students. It was recovered in April 1951 in Scotland. Shortly afterwards it was returned to (but hidden in) the abbey. On 26 February 1952, the stone was replaced under the Coronation Chair. It was padlocked to the chair by means of an inch-thick chain, threaded through the iron loops. There were also warning devices, some of them secret, should anyone attempt to tamper with it again. Police presence in and around the abbey was strengthened in mid-December as a result of information received concerning possible damage to or theft of the stone.

TELEVISION AND THE CORONATION – REACHING THE DECISION

In July 1952 the Coronation Committee, conscious that the Queen was opposed to the idea, concluded that television cameras should be excluded from Westminster Abbey. Churchill, who considered television to be vulgar, was also opposed to its use, as were the Archbishop of Canterbury and the abbey clergy. In particular the Church believed that viewers watching the coronation ceremony over cups of coffee would make it a less dignified occasion. It was also feared that if the procession and service were televised, fewer people would line the coronation route. The preferred idea was for a film to be made which would (presumably suitably edited) be shown to television viewers at a later date. The BBC, the only British television broadcaster at this time, was not consulted over the practicalities of relaying the coronation. Preconceived notions and misunderstandings over how difficult it would be to show the service live (especially regarding issues of lighting and commentary) also contributed to the initial rejection of televising the ceremony announced by the Earl Marshal in October.

Ferranti television and radiogram type TCG1019. This TV and radiogram combination was hardly bigger than a typical television set of the same period. The record deck is positioned above the picture tube to maximise space.

There was, however, considerable public and parliamentary opposition (eighty MPs tabled a motion against the restriction) to the announcement that the coronation would only be broadcast on radio. Consequently the issue was reviewed by committee, cabinet and monarch. In early December the Queen decided that the ceremony could indeed be shown on television. Thereafter, following much discussion and compromise over what was to be shown, the BBC, Buckingham Palace and Westminster Abbey were able to reach agreement. It was decided that the whole day would be given over to the procession and coronation service. The cameras would, however, look away during the anointing and while the Queen took Holy Communion. The cabinet decided that such gaps would be filled by 'symbolic shots' of the altar cross and the nave. Plans were made accordingly. By January, Dr Falkner Allison, the Bishop of Chelmsford, suggested that churches install televisions to show the coronation. No special service should be held, he added; a local church might merely like to provide people with an opportunity to watch the coronation. In February the Queen made her first visit to the BBC.

The certainty and excitement of the coronation being televised led many to decide that now was the moment to buy a set. As a result, 600,000 televisions were sold in 1953 – the first year such sales exceeded those of radios. Some 2,100,000 were licensed. Not all those who sold televisions were necessarily enthusiastic about the sharp rise in demand. One outlet in St Ives, Cornwall, stressed that television was 'still in its infancy' and it could not guarantee reception although it was willing to arrange a (charged) trial installation. Above all, television was not a successor to 'Sound Radio' (a current advertising term) but an 'extra form of entertainment'; a radio was still essential.

Ekcovision television set, model T164, c. 1952. One of the cheaper models, this set still cost around four weeks' wages. By the early 1950s there were over 4 million TV sets in Britain.

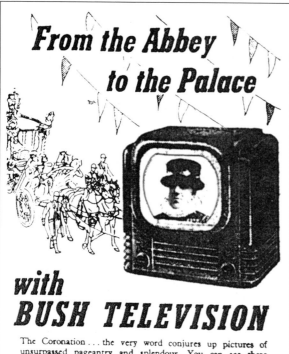

From the Abbey to the Palace with BUSH TELEVISION

The Coronation . . . the very word conjures up pictures of unsurpassed pageantry and splendour. You can see these historic events — see them clearly, realistically — even though the privilege of being present is denied you. Every detail of procession and ceremony can be brought to your home by Bush Television. We will be glad to advise you in the choice of a set and install it in time for the Great Day. Ask for a demonstration of table model **TV. 22.**

THE OFFICIAL REQUIREMENTS AND NATIONAL ASPECTS

Over 100 stamps – one for each colony and dependency – were issued throughout the British Empire to mark the coronation. This was, for instance, Tonga's first new general stamp issue since 1897. The Dominions also had special stamp issues. Those produced by New Zealand were particularly well received. They featured Buckingham Palace, Westminster Abbey and the coronation coach. Two privately owned postal services in the British Isles also marked the occasion later in the year. Herm, a dependency of Guernsey, overprinted their stamps with 'Coronation June 2 1953' and the isle of Lundy, in the Bristol Channel, with 'Coronation 2.6.53'.

Details of the coronation crown coin were released in January. The design was based on the Queen's appearance when she took the Sovereign's Salute at the Birthday Parade on 7 June 1951 wearing the uniform of the Colonel of the Grenadier Guards. The reverse side comprised the four quarterings of the Royal Arms. Each contained a shield and was arranged in the form of a cross. The four national emblems were placed between the shields.

At the beginning of the year peers were invited to apply within days for a maximum of four seats in Westminster Abbey, two of which would have to be paid for. This would be followed by the Royal Summons. There was a ballot for the free seats. Those who did not apply neither received the summons nor were eligible for the free seats. The coronation invitation card was issued in March. This incorporated the Royal Arms, various items of the Regalia and emblems of the Commonwealth. Representing various members of that body, these included roses, thistles, shamrocks, leeks, maples (Canada), wattles (Australia), lotuses (India and Ceylon) and cotton (Pakistan). The design was intertwined with and unified by oakleaves. Some 7,700 invitations were printed and sent out.

Lambeth Council decided that each schoolchild should have a permanent memento of the occasion and commissioned medallions and presentation boxes. (© *Lambeth Archives*)

Another early announcement concerned coronation dress for peers and peeresses and styles for ladies not wearing robes. Ladies, other than peeresses, attending the Coronation were allowed to wear ankle-length dresses with head-dresses consisting of a veil from the crown or back of the head, but it was not to drape lower than the waist. Examples of what the Earl Marshal had in mind were exhibited in the showrooms of the Queen's dress designer, Norman Hartnell.

COMMERCIAL OPPORTUNITIES

As early as March 1952 a Covent Garden company had begun restoring robes which would be hired by peers and peeresses for the coronation. These had been acquired from previous owners and were kept in waterproof boxes in strong-rooms under neighbouring streets. Similarly, the Wilkinson Sword Company reported in January 1953 that it had 2,000 orders for officers' ceremonial swords (which normally cost between £12 and £15) or their replating (£5). It was also receiving about one hundred orders a week worldwide. Taken together, the company was enjoying its best time since 1937 – the year of King George VI's coronation.

The Council of Industrial Design established a Coronation Souvenirs

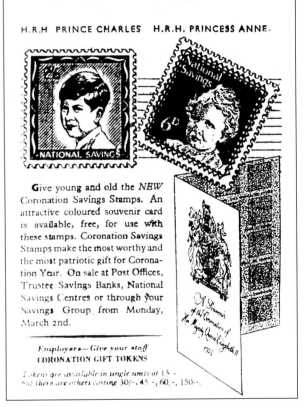

A Memorable Gift for a Memorable Occasion

Coronation Savings Stamps

H.R.H PRINCE CHARLES   H.R.H. PRINCESS ANNE.

Give young and old the *NEW* Coronation Savings Stamps. An attractive coloured souvenir card is available, free, for use with these stamps. Coronation Savings Stamps make the most worthy and the most patriotic gift for Coronation Year. On sale at Post Offices, Trustee Savings Banks, National Savings Centres or through your Savings Group, from Monday, March 2nd.

Employers— Give your staff
CORONATION GIFT TOKENS

Tokens are available in single units of 15/- but there are others costing 30/-, 45/-, 60/-, 150/-.

Committee soon after the date had been announced, and although it was only an advisory body, it hoped to ensure that the commemorative items produced would be of high quality and accurate. Souvenirs sold quite well, and some stores had separate coronation departments. Even so, mistakes occurred: some items showed Prince Philip as a commander, although he had been promoted to the rank of Admiral of the Fleet by June. In March there were reports that the purchase of flags and bunting had exceeded expectations and that there were shortages. This was attributed to the wealthier sections of the population also wishing to have street parties. There was sufficient material but not enough machinists, and it took several months to train someone in the craft of flag-making.

Authorised souvenirs of the coronation.

The committee was also responsible for the thousands of coronation presentation medals struck for and distributed by local authorities to school-children. The harnessing of the event to national well-being, community ideals and individual benefit was seen in another guise – the issue of special presentation holders for coronation year National Savings gift tokens at a time when the savings movement, as represented by various street and group organisations, was thriving.

The coronation influenced advertising in another way too. Moss Bros, the renowned outlet for the hire of clothes, and Guinness were but two of many companies that exploited the event in this way. The Guinness advertisement depicted a zoo-keeper able to hold a bench-full of his menagerie above the heads of a cheering crowd as a result of drinking a glass of this beverage. Above all, the build-up to the event generated something of a holiday atmosphere as people sought to enjoy themselves in different ways. The audiences for Bertram Mills Circus were significantly up at this time, an increase attributed to the coronation. Other circuses and shows also had greater numbers of spectators.

The commercial opportunities presented by the coronation were not limited to Britain. As early as April people in America could buy coronation sweets and salads; coronation dolls and jokebooks (sometimes dedicated to Jackie Gleason and Martha Kaye, 'the King and Queen of laughter'); and coronation carpets and rugs. Coronation tiaras (ranging from 7s to £17,000) were on offer, while costume jewellery manufacturers offered pins and earrings with crown-and-sceptre motifs. There were also coronation buttons, cufflinks and perfume. The American poultry industry sent food writers invitations whereby they were 'commanded to attend the Coronation of Her Majesty Queen Chicken on Coronation Chicken Day'.

LONDON PREPARES

As the centre stage for the grand event, London left nothing to chance. In January the *Illustrated London News* reported the trial runs of coronation decorations which were to feature on street lamps in the centre of the capital. Westminster City Council was responsible for decorations in and over thoroughfares. Hugh Casson acted as the council's consultant. In an address to the English-Speaking Union, he described the coronation as an event similar to Christmas, seeing it as religious and traditional, a national festival and an occasion for a party. He feared the event would be over-commercialised and that television would debase the coronation as a 'solemn religious ceremony'.

Street associations and related bodies devised unified schemes for buildings. The large structures in Regent Street, for instance, were covered with one thousand chrysaline Tudor roses. These were illuminated from within and made a particularly impressive display.

The monarchy proved to be good business for this firm, manufacturing souvenir coronation mugs.
(© *Manchester Central Library*)

Selfridges had a life-size equestrian statue of the Queen behind which was a panel-painting of Elizabeth I. On each side of the display were the promises which the two Elizabeths had made upon their accession. In Trafalgar Square, the bronze statue, capital and panels of Nelson's Column were cleaned and in Piccadilly Circus Alfred Gilbert's *The Angel of Christian Charity* (better known as Eros) was removed to Lambeth for cleaning and repairing. When returned, it was enclosed in a gilded cage. The frontage of King's Cross railway station was also cleaned – for the first time since it had been built in the mid-nineteenth century. There was also a campaign throughout the central area to clean the weather vanes in time for the coronation.

Stands were needed to accommodate the anticipated hundred thousand who would come to watch the event. Some 700 miles of tubular scaffolding were required and, in the interests of economy and to deflect possible opposition to the use of such scarce raw material, the timber required was cut in lengths suitable for re-use in house-building afterwards. The stands' safety was put to the test by 500 volunteer guardsmen and Royal Artillery men who acted as an excess weight test crowd. The earliest stands were constructed in Green Park, the Mall and Hyde Park. Apsley House, the London home of the Duke of Wellington, was practically hidden by those erected around it. Some areas had in due course to be blocked off, but it had been agreed with the police that the boarding used to cover statues and shop windows could be decorated, as were the gates that sealed off certain streets. Tickets for places in the stands changed hands on the black market for £40–£50, while a balcony overlooking the route might cost as much as £3,500.

Access to the centre of London was strictly controlled on Coronation Day. Windscreen labels were available from April for drivers wishing to enter the area. There was parking space for some 15,000 vehicles. Coronation packed lunches in 'decorative cardboard boxes' were also being advertised from this time.

'THE ROYAL HIGHWAY'

This was David Eccles's, the Minister in charge of the coronation, description of The Mall. He believed that these thousand yards from

Buckingham Palace offered 'perhaps the best chance on the route to create that blend of majesty and gaiety which so truly represents our Queen'. Traversing the road were to be four arches of tubular steel latticed in places with fan-shaped designs of gold cane, the twin spans intersecting about 65 feet above the ground. Surmounting each arch were two golden lions and two white unicorns designed by James Woodford. These added a further 20 feet to the height of the arches. Suspended by gold wires from the centre of every arch was a princess's coronet. The four arches were linked by 40-foot standards, which towered above the trees. These standards in turn were surmounted by crowns and hung with four banners bearing the royal monogram. Like the arches, they were to be floodlit at night. The decorations and floodlighting were to remain a feature of London's coronation setting until the middle of June. Special excursion trains, additional coaches and late-night buses (up to 1.30 a.m.) in London itself over this period allowed people to enjoy these illuminations.

Flowers were another feature of the occasion, with some 77,000 red, white and blue plants adding colour to the scene. These included red geraniums and pastel-blue hydrangeas in pots, which were placed around Buckingham Palace and The Mall. The Royal Parks, under Superintendent William Hepburn, were the main provider. He was to have been made a member of the Royal Victorian Order for personal services to the Queen in the Coronation Honours of 1 June, but died the previous day. Flowers were also supplied from elsewhere, including 40 huge boxes from Australia which arrived at London Heathrow on Friday 29 May and were used to decorate Parliament Square.

A sandwich filler for those awaiting the coronation procession.

PREPARING WESTMINSTER ABBEY

The Great West Door of the Abbey was shut to the public in December 1952 until after the coronation, and the remainder of the building was closed the following month. It did not return to its normal state until 1 November. This was because of the preparations and building work, both outside and inside, which needed to be done. A coronation annexe, comprising the royal entrance and great hall, was built against the west front of the Abbey. It was designed by Eric Bedford, Chief Architect of the Ministry of Works, in a style reminiscent of that which had featured at the Festival of Britain.

The annexe cost £50,000 and was made of tubular steel with walls of timber and building-board painted on the outside. Again much of this would later be used in building houses, and it was stressed that none of those involved in the project had been diverted from such construction. On the annexe's walls were the brightly coloured arms and emblems of the Commonwealth, which were also modelled by James Woodford. The side of the annexe facing the main street was lit by a huge glass wall, enabling camera shots to be taken of the Queen after her arrival at the Abbey. The ten 'Queen's Beasts' stood against this front.

THE TEN 'QUEEN'S BEASTS' DECORATING THE CORONATION ANNEXE

The lion of England
The white greyhound of Richmond
The yale of Beaufort
The red dragon of Wales
The white horse of Hanover
The white lion of Mortimer
The unicorn of Scotland
The griffin of Edward III
The black bull of Clarence
The falcon of the Plantagenets

Each six foot high, the beasts in question were heraldic animals holding shields and having, according to the official description, 'expressions of ferocious loyalty on their aristocratic faces'. They were placed in position on 29 May. The canopy was transparent, which helped photographers record the Queen's descent from the State Coach. The turret above the entrance bore the Royal Arms and carried the flagstaff from which flew the Royal Standard while the Queen was in the Abbey.

Inside, 2,000 special chairs and 5,700 stools were required for the ceremony. Those who used the stools could buy them afterwards. Any that remained were to be sold to the public. There was also a 3,000-square-yard chenille Axminster carpet, made at Templeton's mills in Glasgow, Scotland, to be laid. Equipment for television and film coverage of the coronation also began to be installed from December.

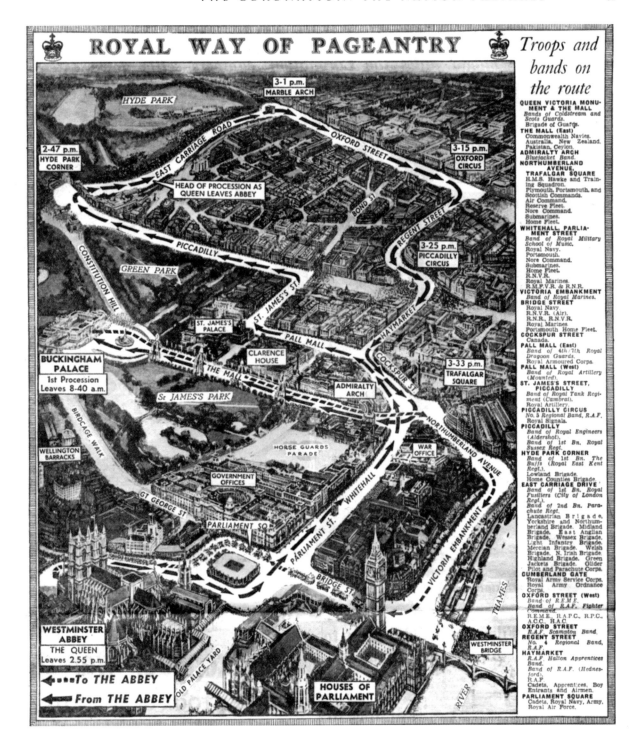

PRACTISING FOR CORONATION DAY

From the *Daily Mail*, Tuesday 2 June 1953.

Those who would take part also had to prepare. Cavalry horses and those from the Royal Canadian Mounted Police were trained under the direction of the Crown Equerry by a unit established at the Royal Mews. Such horses had to become accustomed to noise and excitement. Volunteers from the Royal Veterinary Corps and the Royal Air Force shouted, tins were banged and cloths or handkerchiefs were waved furiously at the animals, which gradually learnt to remain calm in the face of these and other noises, such as bands playing. At their Hendon centre in north London the police practised crowd control. Tall, well-built members of the Metropolitan Force had to withstand the exerted pressure of equally muscular men who played the part of onlookers.

There were two route rehearsals. The first was on Sunday 10 May. Even though the first carriage processions left Buckingham Palace at 5.15 a.m., there were hundreds of people there to watch the practice run. Just over an hour later, at 6.30 a.m., the Second Division's Sovereign's Escort and State Coach left the Palace. It arrived at Westminster Abbey as Big Ben struck seven o'clock, and was greeted by a trumpet fanfare. The longer return journey began an hour later and again the return destination, Buckingham Palace, was reached at exactly the required time. The second rehearsal took place the following Sunday, but at the slightly later time of 7 a.m. This time there were thousands of spectators to watch the practice assembly of the state coaches and carriages at the Palace and Clarence House and their re-assembly with cavalry escorts for the drive back.

There were practices inside the abbey too. On 26 May, forty boys from Eton, Harrow and other public schools, all aged between twelve and fifteen, were drilled in the task of presenting coronets that they were to carry to their masters on the cry of 'God Save the Queen!' after the placing of the crown on the Queen's head. The final rehearsal a few days later, on 29 May, drew big crowds. Mounted police were called to help control the 4,000 people ('mostly women') there and those who gathered for the Changing of the Guard ceremony in the Palace forecourt.

Almost two weeks earlier the Duchess of Norfolk, the wife of the Earl Marshal, had taken the part of the Queen at another abbey rehearsal, although she sat on an ordinary chair. Sir Eric Melville played the part of the Duke of Edinburgh. The Queen's own rehearsals first took place in Buckingham Palace. The ballroom was marked in such a way as to represent the abbey and the Queen used white bedsheets as her coronation train. She also studied film of her father's coronation. She practised several aspects of the service in the abbey itself on 20, 21 and 26 May, including the actual crowning ceremony. The Earl Marshal calculated that this would take place at 12.34 p.m. On the actual day the crown was placed on the Queen's head at 12.33 and 30 seconds.

Preparations for the procession: two Scouts, Jimmy Taylor (nearest camera) of Bow and Michael Sibbs of the Monument, engaged in their bob-a-job task of dusting the wheels of the Lord Mayor's stagecoach, 1953.

PREPARING FOR THE QUEEN

The Imperial State Crown was removed from the Tower of London on 6 January. It was taken to the Goldsmiths' and Silversmiths' Company in Regent Street, where it was prepared for use in the coronation service. St Edward's Crown, only worn at coronations, was worked on in May. The other crown jewels which were required for the ceremony remained on display in the Tower until the end of April.

The Queen was to arrive at and leave Westminster Abbey in two different robes of state: the Royal Robe of crimson velvet on arrival and, after the crowning, that of purple velvet. The latter was made at the Royal School of Needlework in the months preceding the ceremony. The raw silk came from Zoe, Lady Hart Dyke's silk farm in Lullingstone, Kent, and was woven on the hand-loom mills of Warner & Sons, a company based in Braintree, Essex. The robe was embroidered in gold in a design chosen by the Queen based on a motif signifying the hoped-for peace and prosperity during her reign.

Norman Hartnell was commissioned in October 1952 to design the Queen's coronation dress. It was of white satin and similar to her wedding dress, which he had also designed. He submitted nine versions, each with a rose, thistle, shamrock and leek to symbolise the four parts of the kingdom. The Queen decided, however, that the other Commonwealth countries should feature. The accepted design therefore incorporated additionally the lotus (representing Ceylon), protea (South Africa), wattle (Australia), wheat and jute (Pakistan), maple leaf (Canada) and fern (New Zealand). The dress was covered with thousands of tiny seed pearls.

The clergy, too, had to consider matters of dress. Bishops had officiated bare-headed at coronations since the Reformation. But for this coronation it was decided that bishops wearing mitres would look more respectful and avoid camera shots of light-induced sweating.

'CORONATION FEVER'

The coronation was more than a route or ceremony. It had an impact on many aspects of life and provided the theme for various events and activities. These began taking place almost from the start of the year, especially as some of the early social events were to raise funds for spending nearer the time on community celebrations and other ways of marking 2 June itself in the weeks immediately before and after the great day. There were also house-to-house collections. As in St Ives, Cornwall, charities and societies might hold coronation fairs to raise money for their own purposes. It was also the opportunity to organise something different. In Swindon, Wiltshire, there was a

coronation tattoo, a coronation allotments competition and a regatta. Yet in February less than half the population was expected to take an interest in the occasion; by April, however, it was almost 70 per cent. Enthusiasm on the part of the majority only became apparent in the final weeks before 'C-Day'.

Most preparatory events were uncontroversial, but the Yearbook and an invitation card used by the Dudley and Stourbridge Conservative Association in December 1952 aroused the ire of the Dudley Labour MP George Wigg, who argued that it was wrong to use the Queen and the forthcoming coronation for political purposes. Chippenham, Wiltshire, had planned to celebrate the coronation by holding a pig singing contest with a prize of £15. However, this was abandoned in April following protests by the local RSPCA, who were concerned about the suffering and distress which the event would cause the pigs. In Chelmsford, Essex, disputes arose over the choice of the coronation carnival queen. Four of the six unsuccessful contestants refused to be accompanying ladies-in-waiting because the winner had been selected by an unsupervised ballot rather than by popular acclaim.

CORONATION AND FASHION

Princess Margaret, as Patron of the British Colour Council, selected and sponsored coronation colours. Those designated included Marguerite Green, Spun Gold, Princess Grey, Beau Blue and Elizabethan Red. These colours were promoted in various ways, together with suggested uses.

The favourite shades of the summer were rose or pink, albeit there was a coronation nail varnish of green and silver. In women's fashion, there were tiny mock-jewelled coronet hats, mainly in velvet. Crowns were a favourite design theme, along with ideas related to heraldry or 'the Queen's Beasts'. Trains reappeared in Paris, London and Rome dress collections. The coronation had less of an impact on men's fashion, although a coronation tie, featuring a crown picked out in brilliants and gold studs, was produced. There was also a version of the plus-four suit, last popular in the mid-1930s, which incorporated several features of the Norfolk jacket. It was the fancy waistcoat, however, that reigned supreme. Stage, screen and radio celebrities were among the first members of the Waistcoat Club, which was launched in London in November.

More generally, it was noted that the holiday atmosphere in the run-up to the coronation saw many enjoy something of a shopping spree. The press reported women buying 'flim-flams'. These were fluffy dresses in nylons, flowered rayons and silks. Manufacturers feared that prices for nylon dresses would fall in subsequent months.

CORONATION EXHIBITIONS

The Electric Lamp Manufacturers' Association Exhibition in January featured coronation lighting. Displays included equipment for lighting portraits of the Queen from below, and a device which had an exterior pelmet to conceal a fluorescent lamp which lit a window-box planted with flags. There was also a wreath of Tudor roses, surrounded by cardboard laurel leaves and with Christmas tree lamps in their centres.

The Ideal Home Exhibition in March included a Coronation Cavalcade which comprised a two-thirds scale model of the State Coach complete with grey horses, liveried postillions, Yeomen of the Guard, the Standard Bearer and the officers of the Sovereign's Escort. A carpeted route led through the Exhibition to the Cavalcade under canopies of gold cloth edged with ermine and suspended lines of city banners. There was also a Coronation Inn, presented by the Brewers' Society, which acted as a focal and social point for the Village of Ideal Homes. Also topical were the Lion and the Kangaroo fighting for the Ashes – portrayed in Australian butter, a rationed commodity in Britain at the time. The Queen visited the exhibition on 2 March.

The Chelsea Flower Show took place between 19 and 22 May. It included an exhibition organised by the Royal Botanical Gardens which centred around the theme of the Commonwealth. This display comprised typical flora of each member nation together with those of British colonial territories. Many plants were brought to Britain especially for the occasion; some flowers, notably from Western Australia, had to be preserved in ice in order to survive the journey.

In June, Madame Tussaud's re-created the throne room of Buckingham Palace on Coronation Day. Those represented included the Duke and Duchess of Gloucester, the Queen Mother, Princess Margaret and the Princess Royal, the Queen's aunt. There was also an exhibition at the Royal Academy of royal portraits in various artistic forms of most monarchs of the preceding thirteen hundred years. The Bible upon which the Queen took the coronation oath was featured in an exhibition of 'The Treasures of Oxford', which was held in the Goldsmiths' Hall, London.

The Victoria & Albert Museum was disappointed, however, that one of its main displays of coronation year would not be featured. It had hoped to display the Bayeux Tapestry, a near-contemporary depiction of events leading up to and immediately after the Battle of Hastings and the Norman Conquest of England in 1066. Initial discussions with the French authorities were promising but ultimately disappointing when the government refused to allow the tapestry to leave France.

Making ready: a scene typical
of the preparations undertaken
throughout the nation.

PREPARATIONS OUTSIDE LONDON

As 1953 dawned, the newspapers made much of the fact that this
would be the year of the coronation. Coverage was quite extensive,
incorporating both significant and minor details, national and local
ways of marking the event. The New Year's Day issue of the Torquay
Herald Express, for example, reported how earlier that day the local
mayor had planted the first of nine commemorative trees in the
hospital memorial garden. In Croydon the Silver Jubilee of the
Master Bakers' Association featured a replica of the Imperial State
Crown made entirely of marzipan and other sweets. People might
choose, however, to remember the event in a more permanent way.
Mr Wills of Kingsteignton near Newton Abbot presented what was to

become known as 'The 1953 Coronation Trophy'. This was to be awarded in perpetuity to whoever gained the most awards for South Devon cattle in the six major shows at which the breed was exhibited.

Many communities sent elaborate loyal addresses to the Queen – but not St Ives. The town decided instead to use the money which such would have cost to provide a fortnight's holiday for two people living in homes or institutions run by organisations of which the Queen was patron. The Queen viewed this as an 'eminently sensible suggestion' and asked the Town Council to make the choice. The holiday was awarded to a disabled ex-serviceman and his wife, who were welcomed in September by, among others, the Mayor and the Chairman of the St Ives Coronation Committee.

As Coronation Day approached, so the activities became more widespread and impressive. Towards the end of May, Paignton, Devon, organised a 'Pageant of British History' which involved one thousand people and played before three times that number on three successive nights. The final performance was to have been on the twenty-ninth, but the demand for tickets was so great that a fourth show was staged on the following night. However, the local columnist expressed regret that such an event had been ignored in the national press, adding that 'a cat on a roof in Bloomsbury [London] is worth more space than the efforts of a thousand people in the provinces, no matter how important that effort was'.

The religious significance of the ceremony was also appreciated by many people in the days leading up to 2 June. Ten days earlier, Whit Sunday 24 May, was Empire Day, and many linked the two events. For Methodists that date had a further importance in 1953. The year marked the 250th anniversary of John Wesley's birth, while 24 May itself was the anniversary of his religious experience (in 1738) that was to inspire the movement associated with him. On the following Sunday (31 May), many went to church to pray for the Queen. Paignton parish church could accommodate 500 people; 300 worshippers had booked seats beforehand. The church organ played *Rule, Britannia!* before the service began, mingling with the accompanying peal of bells. Other centres held civic services that day. Parades were also a feature over this weekend.

SCOTLAND AND THE QUEEN

While Elizabeth was the second Queen of England to bear that name, her predecessor had not been Queen of Scotland, which was then an independent nation. Therefore, it was argued, her correct title north of the border was Queen Elizabeth I. On 11 February 1952 the Scottish Covenant Association issued a solemn protest over Her

Majesty's title in the territory. Such proclamations declaring her the second Elizabeth over Scotland denied 'the facts of history [and] have flouted the sentiments of Her Majesty's loyal Scottish people'. It went on to say that her advisers appeared to treat them as 'a people subjugated by and made subordinate to the people of England'. In some Scottish towns, after representations by the Scottish Covenant movement, the Provosts omitted from the proclamation any reference to the word 'Second'. In Alva, near Stirling, the prayers identified Elizabeth as the 'First of Scotland and Second of England'.

Such sentiments continued into 1953 and could take a more violent form. Often the appearance in Scotland of the monogram for the new reign ('E II R') generated protests. In November 1952 a new pillar box at The Inch, Edinburgh, was installed. It was the first and for a while the only one with the new cipher in Scotland and was often defaced. On 1 January a postman found an explosive charge. It didn't go off, but one of the letters was charred. Eventually, however, it was shattered by a bomb explosion. The replacement, marked 'temporary', did not carry the offending inscription and thereafter, except on official documents, the numeral was generally omitted from the Queen's title in Scotland.

Princess Margaret in Oxford, attending the wedding of two of her friends.

THE QUEEN'S YEAR BEFORE THE CORONATION

The first part of the year witnessed several 'firsts' for the Queen. The first great social occasion of the year was in January when she, along with the Duke of Edinburgh, Princess Margaret and the Duke and Duchess of Gloucester, was a guest at the wedding of the Earl of Dalkeith, son and heir of the Duke of Buccleuch and Queensberry to Jane McNeill. The ceremony took place in St Giles's Cathedral, Edinburgh. It was the first time a reigning sovereign had attended a wedding in Scotland since before the Act of Union (1707).

The Queen presented the Maundy Money on Thursday 1 April and launched the Royal Yacht *Britannia* later that month. This had been built at the Clydebank shipyard of John Brown. The name of the 4,000-tonne vessel had been a closely guarded secret until then. Even so the band played *Rule, Britannia!* as the yacht headed down the slipway. The Trooping the Colour took place on 7 May.

One of the more poignant occasions of the year for the Queen was the unveiling of the King George VI window which she herself had commissioned for the Queen's Chapel of the Savoy in London. The work of Miss Joan Howson, it featured a portrait of the late king together with a Bible and the lines of Miss Haskin's poem quoted by the King in his Christmas broadcast of 1939. The saddest family event of the year, however, was the death of the Queen's grandmother, Queen Mary.

Mourners at the funeral of Queen Mary, *Daily Herald*, 30 March 1953.

LAST DAYS AND DEATH OF QUEEN MARY

Queen Mary, the widow of King George V (died 1936), was almost eighty-five when Elizabeth came to the throne. For the first time a reigning monarch had her grandmother still living. On the eve of what was to prove her last birthday, Mary revisited her birthplace, Kensington Palace, to examine the coronation robes worn by Queen Victoria. She thought they formed a suitable precedent for the new Queen. Although new robes were made, Elizabeth did wear Queen Victoria's coronation diadem for part of Coronation Day.

Queen Mary was renowned for her knowledge and collection of antiques – often acquired without the owner's willing consent – and recast her will in 1952 so that it encompassed all she possessed and that most items should be passed on to the new sovereign. Her hold on these – and life – remained: not long before her death in March she knew she was losing her memory but, as she told her friend Osbert Sitwell, she meant to 'get it back'.

The aged Queen's health began to deteriorate early in 1953. As she watched London prepare for the coronation she let it be known that should she die before it took place, mourning for her should not delay this solemn and momentous occasion. The end came rather suddenly. Still writing letters within days of her death, she slipped into a coma on the morning of 24 March. Parliament waited anxiously, in the words of the Conservative politician and diarist

Princess Victoria Mary of Teck, the future Queen Mary, in 1884.

Queen Mary, whose 'calm devotion to her public duties . . . never failed over the years', *Daily Herald*, 25 March 1953.

'Chips' Channon, 'for the glorious old girl to die'. So that night did the BBC. As the situation became increasingly serious, the Corporation decided that *The Goon Show* was no longer suitable and should not be broadcast at 9.30 p.m. Light orchestral records were played instead. Queen Mary died at 10.20 p.m. News of her death was first announced when Churchill informed the Commons soon after 11 p.m. and moved the adjournment of the House.

LYING-IN-STATE

On Sunday 29 March Queen Mary's body was brought from Marlborough House to Westminster Hall, where it was to lie in state until the funeral two days later. The procession was watched by thousands all along the mile-long route. Crowds also gathered to pay their last respects in Westminster Hall itself. They began to file past

MOTIONLESS, his halberd reversed, a gentleman-at-arms stands at the head of the catafalque. On top is the Queen's wreath. On the right at the foot of the bier is the flowered cross from Queen Mary's children. On the other side is the wreath from the Queen Mother.

the catafalque soon after 4 p.m. The coffin had a single wreath, comprising lilies-of-the-valley, white freesias and lilies, from Queen Elizabeth with the words 'In loving memory from her devoted Lillibet and Philip'. ('Lillibet' was the name Elizabeth had devised herself when aged two and was much used by her grandparents.) There were two other wreaths nearby. A joint one from her surviving children (the Dukes of Windsor and Gloucester and Mary, the Princess Royal) and daughters-in-law Alice, Duchess of Gloucester, and Marina, Duchess of Kent. The other wreath was from Princess Margaret and the Queen Mother (another daughter-in-law).

Almost ten thousand people had been admitted by 6 p.m. By that time the crowds stretched from Parliament Square to Lambeth Bridge and beyond. As night set in, a sharp wind drove onshore and people protected themselves from the cold. Initially it took about an hour to reach Westminster Hall from joining the queue. However, the crowds were marshalled through the Hall fairly quickly by the police. By midnight it took significantly less time.

On 31 March the coffin was borne through the streets of a crowded, respectful London from Westminster to Paddington station and on from there for the funeral at St George's Chapel, Windsor. After the funeral some of the guests – but pointedly not the Duke of Windsor – were invited to dinner.

Marlborough House, with the blinds drawn after the death of Queen Mary.

The Coronation: The Nation Celebrates

CORONATION HONOURS

Issued on 1 June, the Coronation Honours were a mix of those who were involved in the Coronation and those whose fame was already well established. The arts and sport were particularly strongly represented.

Benjamin Britten, the composer of *Gloriana*, which was to have its first performance as part of the coronation celebrations a week later, was made a Companion of Honour. He was already renowned for his songs, orchestral works, piano and chamber music. His works to date included *Serenade for Tenor, Horn and Strings*, *The Young Person's Guide to the Orchestra*, *Peter Grimes*, *Albert Herring* and *Billy Budd*. Walter de la Mare, poet and author, became a member of the Order of Merit. John Gielgud was knighted. Already a household name because of work on stage and in film, his outstanding achievement in the preceding months was as director of a season of plays at the Lyric, Hammersmith, in London.

Jack Hobbs, the celebrated Surrey, Cambridgeshire and England cricketer, was knighted. Born in 1882, in his first two matches for Surrey in 1905, Hobbs hit 88 against the Gentlemen of England (captained by W.G. Grace) and 155 against Essex, and was awarded his county cap. He had retired in 1934, having scored 197 centuries and played in 61 test matches (41 against Australia). One of the highlights of his career was to score 316 runs not out against Middlesex at Lord's in 1926, an achievement that had yet to be surpassed in 1953. The other great sporting figure knighted was Gordon Richards, the jockey, just a few days before winning the Derby at the twenty-eighth attempt. He had broken the world record, with 4,500 winners less than a year before on 17 July 1952.

FINAL PREPARATIONS

In the early morning of Monday 1 June, accompanied by Special Branch detectives, a lorry travelled from Regent Street to the Dean's

Benjamin Britten with the score of his coronation work, *Gloriana*, which was first performed on 1 June 1953, the eve of the coronation. The Queen attended the opening night at the Royal Opera House, Convent Garden, where Joan Cross played Queen Elizabeth and Peter Pears took the role of Essex.

Yard entrance to Westminster Abbey. It contained the Crown Jewels. They were taken to the Jerusalem Chamber, where they were guarded by Yeoman Warders from the Tower of London until the following day when they were carried in procession to the High Altar and then to the Regalia table.

Late that night Special Branch began a thorough search of giant sewers and cable tunnels which were on the procession route. Other security measures involved detectives posing as programme-sellers and members of the crowds, complete with raincoats, baskets of food, knitting and vacuum flasks. The Coronation Chair was X-rayed to make sure that it was safe and Special Branch guarded the Stone of Scone throughout the night.

LONDON AND THE CORONATION

There were to be a few thousand people in Westminster Abbey and tens of millions throughout the world watching or listening to the great event. In between were the hundreds of thousands on the streets of London. Perhaps the first person to take up her position to watch the coronation was 73-year-old Mrs Zoe Neame, who had started her vigil at 8 a.m. on Sunday 31 May, over fifty hours before the start. She had been training for this at her home and garden (standing there in pouring rain) in Buckinghamshire for the previous six months. The weather forecast for the next two days, showers, meant that she had been wise to do so. Some seven hours later Anne Frances Passey from Surrey sat down at the kerbside in The Mall. Thereafter, especially on the Monday, spectators gradually and increasingly began to take their places.

On the eve of the coronation tens of thousands of people were already waiting on the full procession route, including many Americans and others from overseas (one memorable figure was an Indian chief in full ceremonial dress). An orphan from Winnipeg in Canada was able to see the event because of the kind gift of a restaurant owner in that city. He had won a ticket to London in a bowling contest and, declining the cash alternative, decided to use it in this way. He had been an orphan himself, had memories of a lonely childhood and hoped that his gesture would have a lasting positive impact.

The East Carriage Drive in Hyde Park was much sought after by the all-night campers. The following day, two women scaled the 18-foot wrought-iron Canada Gates in St James's Park. The police made one come down by ladder but the other climbed to the top of the central pillar ('perhaps inspired by the Everest triumph', suggested one news report) and stayed there, 20 feet up. A police officer climbed up, chased her round the narrow ledge at the top but,

CORONATION
OF HER MAJEST

OFFICIAL ROUTE

In addition to the Royal processions, the Lord Mayor of London will leave the Mansion House at 7.55 a.m. to drive in his State Coach drawn by six horses along the Embankment, joining the main Processional route at 8.30 a.m. at Hungerford Bridge, and arriving at the Abbey at 8.45 a.m. Led by the Marshal of the City of London, mounted, and followed by the Lord Mayor's footmen in their liveries, the Lord Mayor will be accompanied by the Lady Mayoress and the Common Cryer with Sword and Mace, and will have an escort of pikemen.

The Speaker of the House of Commons will make the traditional short drive to the Abbey at 9.30 a.m. With him in the Coach will be the Serjeant-at-Arms with the Mace, and the Speaker's Chaplain. There will be an escort of one Life Guardsman and, walking before, the Speaker's Secretary and Trainbearer.

B.B.C. Observers will be stationed at Buckingham Palace, Trafalgar Square, Westminster Abbey and the Annexe, Pall Mall, Marble Arch and Piccadilly Circus. There will be television cameras at Buckingham Palace,

20

From the coronation souvenir programme.

ROCESSION
QUEEN ELIZABETH II

the Embankment, Hyde Park and inside the Abbey. The troops lining the route will be: *The Mall:* Brigade of Guards; *Trafalgar Square to the Abbey and back:* Royal Navy, with Officer Cadets of all three Services in *Parliament Square; Cockspur Street:* Canadian Military Forces; *Pall Mall to Marble Arch:* the Army; and *Oxford Street back to the Haymarket:* Royal Air Force. Below are the approximate times of the return Procession.

	Depart Westminster Abbey	Trafalgar Square	Hyde Park Corner	Marble Arch	Oxford Circus	Piccadilly Circus	Arrive Buckingham Palace
Head of the Procession:	—	—	—	2.55	3.15	3.25	3.45
Her Majesty The Queen:	2.50	3.05	3.25	3.40	4.00	4.10	4.30

Parliament Square on the night of 1 June, showing coronation crowds who had already taken up their positions for the procession the following day.

amid much applause, retired defeated. The woman proceeded to give a running commentary to those below.

Mounted police kept Whitehall and other main thoroughfares clear of what in contemporary terms were described as 'squatters'. But they were allowed to stay at some of the best vantage points where they were causing no obstruction. By 11 a.m. on 1 June, nearly all the kerbside places in Trafalgar Square were occupied (the procession would pass by there three times); The Mall was similarly favoured because here might be seen the morning procession to the abbey and the much longer state procession after the ceremony. To pass the time, people had brought with them portable wireless sets; they also wrote postcards, played games and did crossword puzzles.

Similarly, despite the bad weather, there were newspaper reports of 'people singing in the rain' (echoing the title of a popular film that had been released the year before). The Embankment stands were reserved for 33,000 secondary schoolchildren who would arrive the following day. The London County Council, and Middlesex, Essex, Hertfordshire and Croydon Councils paid the £12,000 it cost for the 28,000 children from their area. Other areas charged the parents: Kent (6*s* per child), West Ham (7*s*), East Ham (7*s* 6*d*) and Surrey (10*s*).

Some people travelled from further afield, taking advantage of special trains early on Coronation Day or during the previous night, such as that from St Ives which left at 7.10 p.m.; a return ticket cost £3 6*s* 3*d*. Similarly, for an excursion fare of 17*s* 3*d*, trains ran from Swindon at 1.35 a.m. (arriving 3.50 a.m.) and 4.30 a.m. (6.10 a.m.).

CORONATION SOUVENIR PROGRAMME

Full details of all those about to pass before the spectators and the service itself were contained in the approved forty-page souvenir programme. This had been issued by the King George's Jubilee Trust on 12 May, the anniversary of the previous, 1937, coronation. The home edition cost 2*s* 6*d*, that for overseas 3*s*; the library edition cost 1 guinea. It was similar in format to the programme produced for King George VI's coronation. Both were overtly imperial, bearing prominently the arms of all the dominions and colonies and listing all the colonial troops present. The programme for 1953 was sold by booksellers and newsagents throughout the country. Consequently those elsewhere could also follow proceedings as the day unfolded on radio and television. The sales' profits went to the Jubilee Trust and were used to the 'advancement

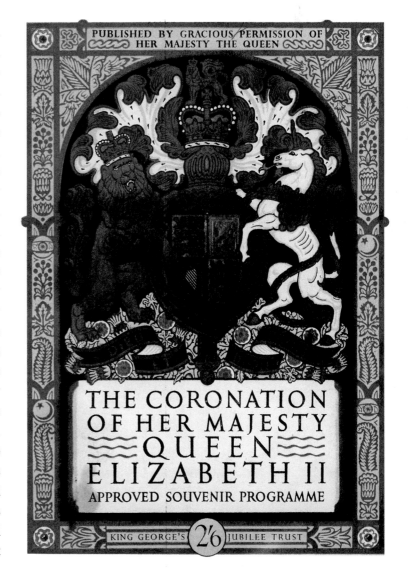

of the mental, physical and spiritual welfare of the younger generation'.

PREPARATIONS AND PROCESSIONS ON CORONATION DAY

There were between 12,000 and 15,000 police on the route. They included 5,000 from 122 police forces from throughout the country. Some slept under canvas in Kensington Gardens; others were quartered at Woolwich. Servicemen were also involved in many ways on the day, including assisting police in traffic control and parking. Their accommodation included the Exhibition Halls of Earl's Court and Olympia. In addition, wartime military camps around London were re-opened, as was the deep air-raid shelter at Clapham Common.

The Navy, Army, Air Force Institute – better known as the NAAFI – provided some 35,000 haversack rations for the coronation troops. The meal comprised a meat roll, a cheese roll, a slice of cake, a bar of chocolate, a packet of barley sugar and an apple. Vegetarians, strongly represented among Asian troops, were given a second cheese roll. Any involvement in the event might receive local press coverage. The *Western Echo* proudly reported that a St Ives national serviceman in the Catering Corps at Aldershot had been selected as one of the cooking staff for the troops in London during the coronation celebrations.

There was certainly much to see, and people began to gather from early in the morning of Coronation Day. At one time people were joining the route at a rate of 4,000 per minute. They could do so partly because public transport was available almost from the start of the day. Most Underground stations were open from 3 a.m. and buses were operating soon afterwards, peaking at 5 a.m. Thereafter roads in the centre began to be closed off and they terminated at some sixteen specified points. London Transport also ran a special 'silver train' to take peers, MPs and guests to the Abbey. It was crowded, with some passengers standing on its first trip from High Street Kensington, to Westminster. It was 6.30 in the morning. Many of the women were in their coronation gowns and the men in court dress. Only one peer wore his full robes with coronet.

At 5 a.m. the Earl Marshal arrived at the abbey. Half an hour later came reporters and cameramen, and the abbey began to fill up soon afterwards, even though people knew they were likely to be there until mid-afternoon. There were press reports that many peeresses brought with them Dorothy bags (a handbag gathered at the top by a drawstring) made in red velvet to match their robes. They kept sandwiches in them to help them through the long wait.

Peers not taking part in the procession were located in the south transept; the peeresses were in the north transept. All of them were seated in rows by order of precedence. By eight o'clock the annexe of the abbey was filling up with dukes, earls, generals and field-marshals. The first members of the royal family – Lord and Lady Harewood with Gerald Lascelles – arrived a few minutes before nine.

The Lord Mayor of London's Procession left Mansion House at 7.55 a.m. It headed along the Embankment, joined part of the processional route towards the end and arrived at the abbey at 8.45. The Speaker of the House left the House of Commons in his carriage at 9.30 for the very short drive to the abbey. A temporary bridge had been constructed the night before to link the Palace of Westminster to Westminster Abbey. Spanning St Margaret Street, it provided peers and politicians an alternative way in, thereby reducing pressure on the main abbey entrance. This idea had first been put into effect at William the Conqueror's coronation on Christmas Day 1066.

A motor-car procession of certain members of the royal family left Buckingham Palace and a similar one of royal and other representatives of foreign states left St James's Palace before 9 a.m. There were four carriage processions, comprising colonial rulers (four carriages), prime ministers (nine carriages), princes and princesses of the blood royal (three carriages) and the glass coach with the Queen Mother and Princess Margaret. In all there were representatives of 72 foreign states, 10 prime ministers and 12 princes and princesses of the blood royal. The Irish Republic chose not to attend the coronation, resenting the Queen of England's claim to sovereignty over *any* part of Ireland and the continued division of that island.

The Queen provided some livery and harnesses, but the Royal Mews did not have enough coaches and carriages. The Hungarian-born British film magnate, Alexander Korda, provided five

AMONG THE FOREIGN REPRESENTATIVES TAKING PART IN THE PROCESSION

Belgium	Prince Albert
Ethiopia	Crown Prince Asfa Wassan
France	Robert Schuman
Iraq	Prince Abdul Illah
Italy	Alcide de Gasperi
Japan	Crown Prince Hirohito
Liberia	William Tolbert
Luxembourg	Grand Duke Jean
USSR	Andrei Gromyko
USA	George Marshall

AMONG THE COLONIAL RULERS AND DOMINION PRIME MINISTERS TAKING PART IN THE PROCESSION

Brunei	The Sultan HH Omar Ali Saifuddin Washa'd Khairi Waddin
Tonga	Queen Salote
Zanzibar	The Sultan Seyyid Sir Khalifabin Harub
Australia	Robert Menzies
Canada	L.S. St Laurent
India	Jawaharlal Nehru
Northern Ireland	Viscount Brookeborough
South Africa	Dr Malan
UK	Sir Winston Churchill
Southern Rhodesia	Sir Godfrey Huggins

broughams and two landaus which had once been used as props. Coachmen were also recruited privately to supplement the regular Buckingham Palace coachmen. The route was not originally to have been sanded because that material was needed for building and was in short supply. However, sand was used on the day, although it was washed away by the rain.

The Queen left Buckingham Palace at 10.26 in the State Coach. The first people to see and greet her were holders of the Victoria Cross and disabled ex-servicemen. She drove the two miles, by way of The Mall, Northumberland Avenue, Victoria Embankment, Bridge Street and Parliament Square, to arrive there almost an hour later. The procession included the Sovereign's Escort of the Household Cavalry as well as over a thousand officers and men of the Brigade of Guards, higher Officers of State and Escorts from the Commonwealth and Colonies. She entered the annexe and, at 11.25, was greeted by the Earl Marshal at the West Entrance; the abbey was full and the Coronation Service about to begin.

THE CORONATION SERVICE AND THE SENSE OF THEATRE

The form and order of this service have altered gradually over the years. A major theme of the four coronations held in the twentieth century (1902, 1911, 1937 and 1953) was the increased emphasis placed on the religious and musical features of the ceremony, with the aim of making it initially much more of a spiritual experience for those taking part. As communications improved, this purpose extended to the congregation as a whole (loudspeakers were first used in the service in 1937) and eventually the wider public, with radio and television coverage.

The heart of the Coronation Service was described by the Archbishop of Canterbury, Lord Fisher, in the souvenir programme, as 'a compact of loyalty between Queen and People and the consecration of the Queen with her people to true service'. There were seventeen parts to the service.

Queen Elizabeth II, wearing the Imperial State Crown, and Prince Philip in the state coach as it turns into the East Carriage Drive of Hyde Park from Piccadilly during the procession from Westminster Abbey to Buckingham Palace after the coronation. Behind are the huge crowds who watched in the pourinng rain, 2 June 1953.

SELECTED STAGES OF THE 1953 CORONATION SERVICE

III	The Recognition
IV	The Oath
V	The Presenting of the Holy Bible
VI	The Beginning of the Communion Service
VII	The Anointing
VIII	The Presenting of the Spurs and Sword
IX	The Investing with the Armills, Stole and Robe Royal and delivery of the Orb
XI	The Putting on of the Crown
XIV	The Homage
XV	The Communion
XVII	The Recess

After making her humble adoration and silent
prayers, Queen Elizabeth II sits in the Chair of
Estate, just beneath the Royal Gallery in which
members of the royal family can be seen,
Westminster Abbey.

The Queen in full coronation splendour.

Queen Salote of Tonga, who attended the coronation and was popular with the crowd.

'The Theatre' was the name given to the great central space in Westminster Abbey where were set three seats for the Queen's successive occupation. Near to the High Altar was the Chair of State; in the middle, facing the Altar, was the Coronation Chair of King Edward I, containing in its base the Coronation Stone of the King of the Scots, which that sovereign had brought back as a war trophy from Scone in 1296. The Coronation Chair was constructed on the orders of Edward to house it. A little further back, approached by five steps, was the Throne. On arrival at the abbey the Queen was led by the Bishops of Durham and Bath and Wells to her Chair of State. These bishops had had that privilege since the time of King Richard I (1189).

In the Recognition the Queen, standing in the middle of the Theatre, was seen and accepted by her people. In the Oath she swore to govern her peoples according to their respective laws and customs. This was followed, before the Altar, by the Presenting of the Bible by the Archbishop of Canterbury and, an innovation in 1953, the Moderator of the Church of Scotland. Such action symbolised the two Churches in particular which the Queen was pledged by oath to protect; she became (and remains) a Presbyterian when north of the border. The Communion Service began but was soon suspended by the formal coronation rituals, starting with the Anointing.

The Anointing was the spiritual climax; in Christian tradition it set the sovereign apart. The Queen had her crimson robe taken from her and sat in King Edward's Chair. Four robed Knights of the Garter held a canopy of cloth of gold over her. Now only the Archbishop of Canterbury could see her as he dipped his thumb in the gilt spoon filled with consecrated oil and held by the Dean of Westminster. He touched the Queen upon her hands, breast and head. In so doing he pronounced a solemn benediction. In stately succession the Queen was then dressed in white and golden vestments. Her hands were touched with the golden spurs of chivalry and the sword. The Archbishop bade her to use the sword to punish evildoers and protect the law-abiding.

The Queen went to the Altar and surrendered to God. More vestments were placed upon her, including the Great Royal Robe, and more of the Regalia presented to her. Another innovation was the revival of the presentation of the Armills or 'bracelets of sincerity and wisdom'. These had been a feature of the ancient rite but had been absent from the ceremony since the seventeenth century. They were the gift of the Commonwealth and seen as a token of its citizens as a whole for the protection and support of their sovereign. She also took up the Orb, symbolising the dominion of the Christian symbol – the Cross – over the world, and received the ring upon her finger. This symbolised that she was wedded to her people. Then she received in her right hand the Sceptre with the Cross (symbolising power and justice) and in her left the Rod with the Dove. This signified that equity and mercy were not to be forgotten. The Crowning followed as the spectacular climax of the Investing.

THE CROWNING

The congregation rose just before the putting on of the Crown, which was placed by the Archbishop of Canterbury upon the altar. He then, together with other bishops, proceeded to King Edward's Chair. The Dean of Westminster brought the Crown to the Archbishop who, in the words of the Coronation Service, 'reverently put it upon the Queen's head'. This was immediately followed by the cry 'God save the Queen!' Princes, princesses, peers and peeresses put on their coronets and caps, bells pealed and the trumpets sounded. Following a given signal, a royal salute of forty-one guns was fired in St James's Park and another of sixty-two guns in the Tower of London.

Rising at last from King Edward's Chair, the Queen was escorted by bishops and peers to be set upon the Throne. There, literally and metaphorically elevated above all others, she received the fealty of the archbishops and bishops, followed by the homage of the lay peers, the first being the Duke of Edinburgh. Thereafter the Communion Service was resumed. Before taking the sacrament, the Queen offered an altar-cloth and an ingot or wedge of gold (weighing one pound). Both were placed upon the altar. Then, having taken off the Crown, she and the Duke of Edinburgh took Holy Communion. Thereafter she received the Crown, Sceptre and Rod and returned to the Throne. A final benediction followed, and the Service ended with the *Te Deum* by William Walton. The Queen eventually left the abbey, to the sound of the National Anthem, wearing the Imperial State Crown of 1838, and bearing the Sceptre and Cross in her right hand and the Orb in her left. The whole ceremony had lasted almost two and a half hours and had witnessed only a couple of minor mistakes.

Daily Sketch, 3 June 1953.

MISSING PERSONS

The presence and involvement of the Moderator of the Church of Scotland was a development welcomed by the Archbishop of Canterbury. Lord Fisher was disappointed, however, that the Roman Catholic Archbishop of Westminster and five Catholic bishops had declined an invitation for their or any Roman episcopal presence at the ceremony. In this the Catholic Archbishop was following the precedent set by former coronations.

Prompted by the Duke of Edinburgh, the Archbishop also suggested that at the Recognition, instead of asking the question four times, he might pose it to different groups – Great Britain and Northern Ireland, the Dominions and the Colonial Empire. However, this was not acted upon because it was too contentious for the Commonwealth Office. Nor was any coronation ceremony, which could have involved representatives of the Commonwealth and Empire, to be held in nearby Westminster Hall. Lord Fisher opposed the restoring of this now severed link.

Finally there was the matter of the Duke of Windsor. In early 1952 he had hoped that he and the Duchess might be invited. But by the end of 1952 this was deemed unlikely and in a press statement, which he had shown to Churchill, he found a dignified way out. He explained that he would be absent because it was unprecedented for any British sovereign or former sovereign to attend such a coronation. Even so, there were rumours in 1953 that he wished to attend and would submit a formal request to Buckingham Palace. The Archbishop made it clear that this was 'wholly and entirely undesirable'. His letters written at the time of his mother's death in March 1953 show that by then he had become alienated from his family (describing them in a letter to his wife as a 'smug, stinking lot'); more generally, he felt that the institution was something of a comic anachronism. Consequently he accepted an invitation from United Press to comment on the ceremony as he watched it on television in the home of American friends in Paris. He was, however, impressed by the Queen's performance at her coronation. In September he wrote *The Crown and the People, 1902–1953*, which drew on and extended the articles which he had written for the British press in the run-up to the coronation.

ONE MAN WHO LOOKED IN

THE Duke of Windsor sat quietly in a room in Paris yesterday and watched the Coronation he did not attend—on TV.

Close beside him sat the Duchess, the woman for whom he gave up the throne. They said little to each other.

Now and then the Duke would explain some detail of the ceremony or identify one of the characters. Those in the room heard that his voice, in the semi-darkness, was husky as if, at times, he found it difficult to talk.

Nine shaded lights cast dim shadows over the room in the house of American heiress Mrs. Margaret Biddle.

The Duke, chain-smoking, started forward when Sir Winston Churchill's face showed on the screen.

"A great old man... a great old man," the Duke said. And he smiled affectionately at the image of the man who stood by him before and after the abdication.

For the Duke it was a journey to a world he once knew.

Excitedly, he pointed out faces he had known since childhood.

THAT IS GOOD . . .

Shoulders touching, and faces almost together, Duke and Duchess sat silently during the Act of Recognition.

And as the cry "God Save Queen Elizabeth" rang through the Abbey, the Duke smiled and said: "That is good."

During the crowning he reached for a handkerchief and brushed his solemn face.

Then he turned towards his wife and pinched the flesh between his eyes in the gesture that a man uses when he fights back a tear.

From the *Daily Sketch*, 3 June 1953.

AFTER THE CEREMONY

The Queen remained in the annexe with the Duke of Edinburgh and other members of the royal family to enjoy the luncheon which had been brought by Palace footmen about eight hours before. The Queen was toasted in champagne; she drank only water. She remained there longer than expected – partly because, it was rumoured, Churchill had suggested a delay as he was convinced that the sun would come out.

By the time the Queen re-entered the State Coach outside Westminster Abbey in the predicted glorious sunshine, the full state procession, extended by contingents of the armed services with

Procession headed by Princess Alice of Greece (mother of the Duke of Edinburgh) leaving Westminster Abbey after the coronation.

detachments from the defence forces of the Commonwealth and Colonies, had formed its head at Stanhope Gate in Hyde Park. Predominantly military, it comprised 16,100 from the Army, 7,000 from the RAF, 3,600 from the Navy, 2,000 from the Commonwealth and 500 from the Colonies, who either took part in the procession or lined its route. There were also twenty bands along the full procession route and a further twenty-nine in the procession itself. It took forty-five minutes to pass and went by way of Oxford Street, Regent Street, The Haymarket and back along The Mall. It was a five-mile progress from Westminster Abbey to Buckingham Palace.

Among the most memorable of the participants was Queen Salote of Tonga, wearing an impressive head-dress of twin egret feathers and accompanied in the carriage by the Sultan of Kelantan. The only other figure in Whitehall to be officially acknowledged as Her Majesty, she was also held in high esteem by the crowds. Setting off before the Queen, she had ignored the frequently heavy rain and rode in an open carriage followed by an escort of mounted military police. The Churchills were forced to halt outside Canada House because of the risk of collision with another carriage. Having lost his place in the procession, Churchill withdrew and returned to Downing Street.

One million people were thought to be on the processional route, but there were less than 7,000 casualties. Some people had legs broken in the crush; others suffered exposure after spending the night on wet pavements to make sure of a good view. Over 300, however, were taken to hospital. Six soldiers were injured by fixed bayonets.

The Queen's return to Buckingham Palace had been timed for 4.30 but the procession was behind schedule, in part because of the delayed start. But also the pace was slowed as horses began to slip in the rain-washed roads. Once the Queen was inside the palace the crowd surged forward against the gates and roared for her to appear. She remained inside for a while, among other things, awarding Prince Charles a coronation medal. It was his first decoration. After family photographs by Cecil Beaton, however, she appeared on the balcony. This was not so much in response to the crowd's demands below as in anticipation of the pending (if, because of adverse weather, modified) fly-past. It featured twelve squadrons of RAF Meteors and two of Royal Canadian Air Force Sabre jets; two squadrons at a time at intervals of thirty seconds.

During the course of the rest of the day and into the night, the Queen made six balcony appearances before crowds of at least 150,000. One, at 9.45 and still amidst pouring rain, involved her switching on a river of light: the arches in The Mall lit up and Nelson's Column was floodlit. After the first cheerings over such delights, the crowds fell silent to listen to the Queen's coronation broadcast from Buckingham Palace to the Commonwealth, which concluded by thanking everyone for their loyalty and affection. The crowd stood bareheaded in the rain as the National Anthem was played.

Finally, on three hundred yards of the South Bank of the River Thames there was a fireworks display, culminating in pyrotechnic displays of images of the Queen, the Duke of Edinburgh, Prince Charles and Princess Anne. The display, it was claimed, could be seen ten miles away. It proved a fitting climax to a memorable day and occasion.

The Royal Gallery: Prince Charles looking unusually solemn standing between Queen Elizabeth the Queen Mother and Princess Margaret watching his mother the Queen being crowned.

CELEBRATING THE CORONATION OUTSIDE LONDON

The most popular forms of marking the occasion were presentations of souvenir beakers or mugs to and/or outings for children under sixteen, special meals or entertainments for the elderly and street parties. At Torquay parents and children queued outside the town hall, where the mugs were distributed by the local Women's Voluntary Service. To prevent abuse (as happened elsewhere), each child's ration book was stamped 'mug received'. The souvenir was glazed with a finish inscribed with the borough arms, the coronation emblem and a portrait of the Queen. Some 11,000 mugs were distributed in this area.

Babies born in Wales on 2 June were each given a silver spoon; those born in Chippenham, Wiltshire, were given a new crown piece. At the hamlet of Bayden, also in Wiltshire, sports events were organised for the children and a tea held for 250 residents. The elderly and sick each received a parcel of groceries. The older residents of Crudwell, Gloucestershire, were given tea and supper

A typical coronation street party.

but were asked to bring their own cutlery, as none remained for hire. There were also competitions for the best-decorated house. The owner of a house in Purton, Wiltshire, displayed a model of the Coronation Coach and St Edward's Crown, made from icing sugar and covered with gold powder.

Hastings began its coronation celebrations at 6 a.m., other places slightly later. The firing of maroons was a popular way of starting the day, perhaps followed later with a 21-gun salute. Householders in the vicinity were often advised to keep their windows open to reduce the risks of blast damage. The other sound was the pealing of church bells, often combined with an early morning service. There was morris dancing at Watton Hall Park in Liverpool. But not all public ways of marking the day were necessarily official. Silver Street Bridge, Cambridge, had overnight been painted red, white and blue. Undergraduates were thought to be responsible. In Sutton, Surrey, the first 15 feet of a chestnut tree were still in full red blossom. Thereafter the blossoms were white. A young boy climbed to the top and decorated it with blue streamers.

The nation took to the street on Coronation Day with bunting, homemade cakes, sandwiches and (sometimes) fancy dress. The party held in Chesterton Hall Crescent, Cambridge, was typical of many being celebrated elsewhere. The road was closed at both ends, games and races held and a memorable tea provided, culminating in a fairly large cake. This was a joint effort, with people pooling

There were hundreds of coronation parties such as this all over Britain in June 1953.

Swinbrooke Road, Kensington, London, with 253 children enjoying the celebrations, for which the organisers had collected £570. Besides bus tours of the coronation route and a show that included conjurors and clowns, there was a feast with a 60lb cake and every child received a 15s Savings Certificate. The 'Queen' was fourteen-year-old Maureen Atkins.

rations and contributing to the success of the day. Two neighbours there, Gladys Nightingale and Gwen Warrington, had agreed to ice the cake following a recipe which had featured on television. It was difficult to get the right red and blue icing, and there was disagreement over how the cake should be decorated but 'E II R' and the date, in a rather pale pink and blue, won the day. In Poona Road, Tunbridge Wells, the day was rounded off with fireworks, but they all went off together when the person in charge dropped a lighted cigarette on them – much to the disappointment of the young children, who had been allowed to stay up to see the display.

Local celebrations continued into the evening, with such delights as roasted ox (Finnish reindeer in Symonds Yat), coronation television balls (a mix of dancing, viewing of the coronation telefilm and the broadcast of the Queen's address that night) and fireworks. There was a change of location for the display at St Ives. The lakeside of the park there was no longer available and a car park was used instead. This was because a few days before the event nine cygnets had been hatched at the lake. There was also a chain of impressive bonfires built and lit by boy scouts around Britain. At 10 p.m. a rocket from Wolf Rock lighthouse off Land's End gave the signal for bonfires to be lit throughout Cornwall and beyond. That on Hillsborough Hill, outside Ilfracombe, Devon, had had to be hastily rebuilt as it had caught fire on coronation eve. The displays could be quite impressive – the one at Brocklesby in Lincolnshire was 35 feet high and soaked in one hundred gallons of old tractor oil. At John o' Groats, the northernmost part of Scotland, the bonfire was lit by a flaming branch that was carried in a 5-foot torch-holder first used to light the coronation bonfire for Queen Victoria in 1838.

SNAPSHOTS OF OVERSEAS CELEBRATIONS

Lighthouse families at Gabo Island, Australia, were forbidden to hang out flags. So instead, to mark the occasion, they hung red, white and blue washing on the line. In South Africa aeroplanes flew over Pretoria in a letter 'E' formation, while in Canada the Governor-General, Vincent Massey, took the salute from more than 6,000 servicemen in Ottawa in front of about 100,000 others.

The coronation took place during Ramadan, but Moslem children under fifteen in Selangor State, Malaya were allowed to eat cakes and have drinks at parties held there to celebrate the event. Elsewhere in Malaya, Buddhists in Ipoh held a special meeting to pray for 'the long and glorious reign' of the Queen.

In Korea on Coronation Day the Commonwealth division artillery fired a 101-gun salute. The guns were pointed towards the enemy but were plotted in such a way that the shells did not hit anyone. In Moscow the Russian Foreign Minister attended a coronation banquet at the British Embassy and proposed the toast, which was drunk in champagne. In the town of Shataukok, which comprised a single street, half celebrated with tea, cakes and fireworks, the other half could merely look on. This was because part was in British territory, while the other half, across the frontier from Hong Kong, was in the People's Republic of China.

MEDIA COVERAGE OF THE CORONATION

There was extensive press coverage of the event, with local and national newspapers both bigger than normal, issuing more editions on the day and often incorporating a crown in their masthead. Some local papers anticipated distribution problems and some were sold without vendors. The Torquay *Herald Express* urged its readers to 'Just help yourself . . . and drop 2d in the bag. We trust you'. It was estimated that some 2,000 journalists and 500 photographers world-wide covered the event. The *Chicago Tribune* printed what it described as the first colour photograph of the coronation to be published anywhere in the world. The photograph was eight columns wide and almost half a page deep. It showed the State Coach turning into The Mall.

But it was radio, cinema and above all television which transformed the number of those who could follow and indeed see something of the 1953 coronation. From being an essentially London event, it became a global phenomenon. Some 140 commentators speaking at 104 commentary points described the ceremony in over 40 languages. Twenty-two countries received simultaneous commentary of part or the whole of the day's proceedings, while recorded accounts were relayed to a further thirty-seven countries. The BBC World Service broadcast a total of 391 hours from 38 short-wave transmitters to the Commonwealth and elsewhere.

The BBC played a crucial role in making all this possible. From the beginning of 1953, it carried out tests for television relays to continental Europe. It also set up temporary radio links to enable television programmes to be relayed by local stations in France, The Netherlands and the then Federal Republic of Germany. This involved, among other things, converting its 405-line picture form to that of 819 lines (for France) and 625 lines (The Netherlands and Germany). The television audience in continental Western Europe for the coronation totalled 1.5 million.

The RAF and the Royal Canadian Air Force also played an important role. There was as yet no live transatlantic television transmission. Therefore, as the day unfolded, viewers in Canada and the USA could only look at a succession of still photographs transmitted by wire, changing every two minutes and accompanied by live commentary. RAF helicopters took the television recordings of the coronation at two-hourly intervals to one of three waiting Canberra PR3 jet bombers. They in turn flew them to Goose Bay, Labrador, in just over five hours. The film was processed and edited on board. Canadian CF-100s flew the film on to Quebec. Two American networks, NBC and CBS, tried to fly their own tele-recordings to the USA. But the plane turned back because of engine trouble and NBC used the last RAF Canberra to transport the film to North America. Mustang fighters took the film to its American destination. Two million Canadians watched the coronation; in the USA the figure was 85 million. The coronation was the top-rated US and Canadian television production of the year.

BRITISH TELEVISION AND THE CORONATION

From its evolution in the 1920s, the BBC had revered the Crown. In Richard Dimbleby the Corporation had found the appropriate voice and attitude. In 1939 Dimbleby had been sent by the BBC to cover King George VI's and Queen Elizabeth's tour of Canada. This was the first royal tour accompanied by the BBC, and Dimbleby was congratulated by its Board of Governors for his 'outstanding' coverage. By 1953 his respect for the institution of monarchy had become a matter of devotion. By then, as a result of war reporting, victory parades, a royal wedding and innumerable state occasions, his tone in covering such events was much admired.

At the 1937 coronation, there had been seventeen sound-commentary positions along the route; television had three cameras, all operating from Hyde Park Corner. In 1953 there were ninety-five sound-commentary positions and twenty-one cameras (five of which were in the abbey). Dimbleby had experience in both radio and television outside broadcasting and was approached by both. He was chosen by *Sunday Graphic* readers as the preferred coronation television commentator, easily beating John Snagge, Howard Marshall, Frank Gillard and Wynford Vaughan-Thomas. The Corporation also opted for Dimbleby; John Snagge broadcast for the radio, assisted by John Arlott.

Dimbleby spent six months preparing for the coronation and became totally immersed in its history, meaning and timings. Consequently, in view of the May rehearsals, he could prepare commentaries that would fit into the times available. For ease of access, he chose to live on a Dutch sailing barge on the Thames just before

Richard Dimbleby and his wife and children in the 1950s.

the event and on 2 June itself had a police launch escort to the steps of Westminster Pier. At 5.30 a.m. he occupied his commentary position high up in the triforium, looking down on King Edward's Chair. He sat in a little glass, sound-proofed box, feeling very nervous. At 10.15 a.m. Sylvia Peters opened the proceedings for television and seven commentators watched the coronation procession on its way to the abbey. Dimbleby had a final glance through the notes which had been prepared and extensively rewritten in the preceding months. He was much moved by the ceremony and his commentary was heard and well received throughout the world. Similarly, the British press and others were enthusiastic over Dimbleby's coverage.

The significance of television – especially live outside broadcasts – was for the first time fully appreciated. Its coverage of the Coronation had set a standard but also created the expectation that other royal events would be televised. On the afternoon of the coronation the BBC decided that Dimbleby should return to the now silent and near-empty abbey later that evening and provide a reflective postscript. He did so, leaving soon after midnight – seventeen hours after first entering it.

Royal visit, June 1953: Queen
Elizabeth II and Prince Philip
driving through Lambeth.
(© *Pat Smith*)

It was estimated that nearly half the population watched the
coronation on television. Prisoners in Exeter jail did so, while those
in St Marychurch could see it at the town hall. This cost 15*s* but
included a buffet lunch. The home, however, was the focal point,
with friends and neighbours often invited in to enjoy the occasion.
Television therefore added to the sense of community which proved
such a feature of the coronation celebrations, although several
people in front of a small screen might mean that not everyone had
an unimpeded view. Furthermore, notices appeared in local
newspapers urging motorists and users of electrical equipment such
as hair dryers not fitted with suppressors to avoid using them during
the coronation broadcast. These were not problems for those who
saw television coverage of the coronation – at their local cinema.
The cinemas picked up the ordinary BBC transmission with roof
aerials and relayed the proceedings on large screens. Some 2,500
watched the coronation in this way at the Odeon, Leicester Square,
London. Nearly 18,000 more were able to do so in other cinemas in
London, Manchester, Leeds and Doncaster. A cinema in Düsseldorf,
Germany, also offered the same.

AFTERMATH

The Queen's coronation robes went on display in St James's Palace for just over a month from 10 June while the Abbey itself retained its coronation setting for a while so that people might see it for themselves. For a few days immediately after the event some cinemas showed only the coronation newsreel at a reduced admission price. Soon, however, *A Queen is Crowned* and *Elizabeth is Queen Today* (described as 'the full-length Coronation film') were on general release.

THE ARTS AND THE CORONATION

The music for the coronation was under the direction of Dr (later Sir) Willian McKie, the organist of Westminster Abbey, assisted by Sir Arnold Bax, the Master of the Queen's Musick. Unlike the liturgical forms, the music is chosen anew for each coronation. That of 1902 sought to feature English music of every age, especially contemporary composers. The same idea was pursued in 1953. The service included work by Handel ('Zadok the Priest'), Sir Hubert Parry ('I was Glad') William Walton (a setting of the *Te Deum*) and Vaughan Williams's setting of the Old Hundredth ('All people that on Earth do dwell'). The anthems were representative of those written between the reigns of Queen Elizabeth I and Queen Elizabeth II, and included work by Orlando Gibbons, Samuel Wesley and a specially commissioned work by the Canadian Healey Willan.

Sadler's Wells Ballet performed *Homage to the Queen* on 2 June. This was choreographed by Frederick Ashton, with music by Malcolm Arnold. Among those taking part were Margot Fonteyn and Beryl Grey. On 8 June there was the first performance of Britten's *Gloriana*. The Arts Council commissioned *A Garland for the Queen*, which received its first performance on the eve of the coronation. It was a collection of ten songs by a mix of living composers and poets. The Council was also prominent in its support for the St Ives Festival of music and the arts. A first, it took place between 6 and 14 June and was on a par with those held in Edinburgh, Aldeburgh and Bath. The idea of St Ives as a festival centre had been originated by Priaux Rainier and Michael Tippett (both of whom were musical advisers), together with local resident Barbara Hepworth.

The coronation also had an impact on popular music. Compositions which appeared at this time included *The Windsor Waltz*, *1953 Coronation Waltz*, *Coronation Samba*, *Coronation Rag* and *Britannia Rag*. Leon and Malloy's *In a Golden Coach* ('There's a Heart of Gold'), sung by Donald Peers, evoked the coronation without mentioning it directly.

THOSE NOT CELEBRATING THE CORONATION

A group of Scottish Nationalists gathered around the Market Cross in Aberdeen just as the Queen was about to be crowned. But not in order to honour the event. Their purpose was, in view of 'the unfounded English claim to the overlordship of Scotland', to declare 'the new Scottish Republic'. In Largs, the Scottish Republican Army damaged the coronation decorations in the municipal offices. Members had cut the 'II' from the banner with the Queen's cipher 'E II R'. In Dublin, the Union Jack was burnt after a protest march against the naming of Elizabeth as Queen of Northern Ireland. Elsewhere a coronation television party was broken up by a man who smashed the set with an axe. Some fifty British servicemen were ejected from a hotel in Houston, Texas, for singing *Rule, Britannia!* too loudly and residents in Lemoyne, Alabama, protested when the Union Jack was flown from a local factory.

Finally, there were certain criminals who did not know about or observe the great occasion. Jewellery worth around £50,000 was stolen from the safe at the home of the Duke of Sunderland in Knightsbridge, London, during the early hours of 2 June. The theft was discovered by the Duchess as she, the Duke and their guests were about to leave for Westminster Abbey. Fortunately they still had their coronets, as these had been kept elsewhere. A beggar appeared before Croydon Magistrates' Court and said that he did not know that it was Coronation Day. The chairman of the bench, while acknowledging that the person's record was not good, nevertheless decided that it was 'a day of rejoicing'. He was therefore given an absolute discharge and left the court without further penalty.

THE QUEEN'S YEAR AFTER THE CORONATION

In the weeks following the coronation, the Queen undertook various tours of her kingdom. In addition there continued to be celebrations and special events to mark the occasion. There was a Thanksgiving Service in St Paul's on 9 June, a Review of the Fleet at Spithead less than a week later, and a royal river pageant on the Thames. The Queen also attended a coronation review of 72,000 ex-servicemen and women. A memorial to the Commonwealth airmen who had died in the Second World War was unveiled at Runnymede near Windsor in October. In November the Queen opened Parliament and attended the Remembrance ceremony at the Cenotaph. Shortly afterwards she and the Duke of Edinburgh began the Royal Tour.

Postponed in 1949 because of King George VI's illness and interrupted by his death in February 1952, the six-month tour – with

TUESDAY, JUNE 16. 19[

EET UNDER AN UMBRELLA OF ROCKETS

Australia and New Zealand as the highlights – began again on 23 November. The first week was spent in Bermuda and Jamaica. During a farewell parade at Port Royal, a Jamaican recalled Sir Walter Raleigh's example when he spread his jacket at the Queen's feet. The royal party travelled on to Fiji and Tonga, where they were hosted by Queen Salote. On 22 December they sailed for New Zealand, spending Christmas and New Year in that country.

The Review of the Fleet at Spithead on 15 June 1953, with rockets arching over the illuminated ships to provide an umbrella of fire, *Evening Standard*, 16 June 1953.

Work and Leisure in the Home

THE IDEAL HOME ON DISPLAY

The thirtieth Daily Mail Ideal Home Exhibition was held at Olympia, London, from 3 to 28 March. The village of Ideal Homes displayed six houses and two flats. They were located around the Women's Institute's Country Market. It also had fourteen shops selling products displayed elsewhere in the exhibition. The Ministry of Housing and Local Government had the largest exhibit, which included a two-bedroom house, a three-

The Daily Mail Ideal Home Exhibition at Olympia, the previous year.

Prefab housing with well-kept gardens, Clapham Common, London, 1953.

bedroom house and a pair of two-storey cottage flats. One of the flats was furnished while the other was deliberately left empty in order to demonstrate the alternative materials and methods which could be used for the construction of interiors. Building costs were three times higher than before the war, so new methods and materials could help counteract this. It was estimated that the inside of a house took twice as long to build as the walls and roof.

The two-bedroom 'People's House' was intended for a family of four including two-year-old twins. The furniture and fittings on display cost £485, or around £550 if bought on hire purchase. They were often from the cheaper range – the total cost of the settee and two easy chairs was £63 7s 6d. There was also the Unity House, which had three bedrooms and made much use of prefabrication, both for the external framework and internal features. It cost £1,250. Orders for houses could be booked on the spot.

THE HOUSING REALITY

The housing shortage in the immediate postwar era loomed large in many people's minds. The Labour government had looked to and helped local authorities to provide housing for rent. When Labour

Mr Harold Macmillan, Minister of Housing and Local Government, making a speech as he opened new houses built by non-traditional methods in Eastcote, Ruislip.

left office in 1951, less than 20 per cent of houses built since 1945 had been for owner-occupiers. The successor Conservative government placed greater emphasis on home ownership and the Minister for Housing, Harold Macmillan, promised 300,000 new houses a year. By August 1953, some 25,121 houses were built, and his goal was now in the process of being achieved. Such success was partly because the Conservatives' 'People's House' had an area of 900 square feet while the equivalent Labour house had over 20 per cent more.

In this year, too, restrictions on new buildings ceased and, for the first time since 1939, houses could be constructed without the need to obtain building permits. In the eight years since the war, over 1.75 million permanent houses had been built by local authorities, housing associations, government departments and private builders. Even so, the continuing high marriage rate meant that many young couples in 1953 (and after) started married life living with parents, usually the bride's.

KEEPING HOUSE

According to the 1951 census, little more than 1 per cent of households had resident servants. Those, predominantly middle-class, housewives who perhaps before the war had traditionally limited their activities to the drawing room and dining room now found themselves with the tasks of cooking, washing and cleaning which had previously been carried out by others. The kitchen was the centre of household activity and women, who used it most, wanted it to be skilfully planned and equipped with 'labour-saving' devices. Working-class women were similarly minded and were gradually able to afford what they wanted.

By 1953, four out of five households had a gas supply, and around 90 per cent were wired for electricity. In addition to these developments and the expansion of mass production techniques, a modern kitchen was increasingly realisable as a result of near-full male employment and more opportunities for, and the greater acceptance of, married women pursuing paid work outside the home, even if wage inequality persisted and much work was part-time. Furthermore, hire purchase was now widely available, less onerous and more socially acceptable. Mail order was another way to spread payments. Burlington Credit Mail Order, based in Manchester, had been launched in 1952; Brian Mills of Sunderland followed in 1953. Even so, pre-war consumption of many goods (and indeed some foodstuffs) was not surpassed until the mid-1950s.

The fitted electric or gas cooker now replaced the cooking range and might be accompanied by a double sink and laminated furniture. The multi-purpose cabinet was also a much-favoured feature, either in its natural state or painted. Shelves and compartments would be found behind a dropped-down or pull-out enamelled flap. There might also be storage jars and ventilation grilles for storing fresh food. The larder would also be used in this way and was often situated on the north or east side of the kitchen, with a stone or tiled floor. Small units with wire-mesh doors might be placed here and used for storing meat. Gradually, however, homes were acquiring gas or electric refrigerators which made, according to the advertisements, 'once a week' shopping possible. Frozen food and vegetables were also available, although fewer than 100,000 packets were bought in 1953.

Cooking food was made easier by the greater availability of thermostatic controls on both gas and electric ovens. Advertisements would feature housewives alongside such equipment and surrounded by food, implying perhaps that the appliances had done the preparation too. Electric food mixers, coffee percolators, pressure cookers, food blenders, dishwashers, vacuum cleaners, heaters and washing machines were similarly marketed as reducing the housewife's burdens or enhancing the family's lifestyle. Marketing of such goods achieved national and political prominence in December 1953. A display at that time in the Electricity Board showroom in Warrington, Lancashire, featured the Three Wise Men bearing gifts of an electric cooker, a refrigerator and a washing machine. The House of Lords debated the various implications of such commercialism.

'Who couldn't cook well in a kitchen like this?' A couple happily preparing a roast in an advertisement for the paint company Robbialac.

EATING

The emphasis on the kitchen and food preparation was understandable. Eating was still an essentially domestic, family activity which, because most of the food was prepared at home, shaped the day. School meals and works canteens were well-established features by 1953, yet most children and a majority of men returned home for a midday meal. Even those men who ate away from home often took food which had been prepared for them earlier that day or the night before and taken in a lunchbox; the first cling film designed for household use appeared in 1953. In such cases they expected to return home to 'a proper meal', which would usually involve other members of the family. This was even more so on a Sunday. The main meal that day was often the best of the week and in abundance (often, usefully, forming the basis of what would be eaten the following day).

Meals could take quite a while to prepare, as there were few convenience foods. With less than 5 per cent of households owning a refrigerator, daily shopping for food was the norm. Tinned vegetables helped out but were looked upon as inferior by many families. Most bought (and many grew their own) fresh produce. Similarly, when sugar ceased to be rationed in September, people once more began to make jam or bottle fruit in syrup rather than in water. Ice-cream was a popular convenience food, but few could store it in a refrigerator. Consequently Wall's advertisements explained that provided they were well wrapped in newspaper when bought, their blocks of ice cream would stay firm for two to three hours, by which time they would be ready for eating.

There might also be late afternoon or early evening tea, comprising sweet or savoury sandwiches, tinned fruit and home-made cakes. Recipes were a regular feature of women's magazines and soon became more imaginative and generous. In February, with the end of sweet rationing, recipes for real chocolate icing, chocolate cakes and desserts were much in demand. The following month eggs came off ration – dried eggs had been a welcome substitute, but not everyone enthused over them. They made an acceptable soufflé, but the dish tasted much better when made with fresh eggs. In April real cream became available again. This had not been rationed: it was illegal for farmers to produce it for sale. One convenience which first became widely known in 1953 was the teabag, although it had been invented in 1908. Tetley sold them in America in the 1930s but it was only in this year that the Tetley teabag was formally launched in Britain.

Tea remained the nation's favourite drink, but coffee, especially in light of men's wartime experience, had a growing market. The espresso coffee machines were gradually being established, having first been imported in 1952. Coffee bars already enjoyed some popularity.

WASHING

Household laundry could dominate the week. Monday was washday for most people, as washing, wringing, drying (especially) and ironing might need several days. Fewer than one in six households had a washing machine at this time (although they could be rented for a few shillings per morning), and most of these were little more than wash-boilers. Those who washed by hand might use a corrugated wood, glass or metal washboard, which stood in a tub or 'posser' of hot soapy water. The clothes were then rubbed against its ribbed surface. A washing dolly – a wooden object shaped like a stool

Kitchen and washing-machine of 1953.

with several legs attached to a long handle – might also be used. Clothes, water and soap were put into a barrel-shaped dolly tub. The dolly was moved about, pummelling the clothes rather like the action of an early washing machine.

As most household fabrics were cotton or linen, boiling was the preferred way to keep them clean and fresh. This might be achieved by mixing washing soda and grated ordinary soap, or using pure soap flakes. But soap powders such as Persil, Rinso, Tide, Oxydol and Daz (launched 1953) were already on the market, as were Dreft, Lux and Paddy, the last a speciality of the soap works owned by the Co-operative Wholesale Society. After the articles had been boiled they would be placed in the sink, often with the aid of large wooden tongs, then rinsed several times. Inadequate rinsing caused whites to become grey; excessive use of soap made them yellow. Similarly, starching of clothes and household linen was commonplace but needed to be done carefully or else the item would become too stiff for use. Care also had to be taken when rinsing in blue or 'blueing the whites'. The aim was to enhance the whiteness; the agent was only to be used in the final rinse. Users were often anxious about the amount required, fearing that too much would colour the garments, although only temporarily.

Wringing was done by hand. During school holidays at least, children might assist by lifting the heavy washing out of the sink and into a galvanised tin tub. Perhaps too they would feed the washing into the wringer and turn the handle. Washing might also be sent out to laundries or to those who 'took in' washing. Some towns also had launderettes.

With less than 1 per cent owning a tumble dryer in 1953, 'a good drying day' was a welcome sight on regular washdays but it would also be an opportunity for washing such occasional items as blankets, which was a particularly exhausting task. Washing would be hung in

the garden to dry. Families without gardens, especially in industrial areas, often hung washing across the street. In bad weather laundry was dried indoors. Many used a clothes horse in front of a (coal) fire, which might cause windows to steam up. Once the washing was dry, the next and final task would be the ironing. Flat and gas irons were still in use, but electric irons had appeared before the war. Flat irons were heated up and the temperature gauged by applying a moistened finger. Gas irons might be heated on a gas burner; modern models of the time had an integral burner, with the gas supplied by a flexible tube. Often electric irons had long flexes so that they could be plugged into ceiling light sockets as homes did not necessarily have sufficient power points.

Above, left: Persil had just come on the market in 1953. *Right*: Backyard washing in the 1950s.

CLEANING

Many continued to believe that 'cleanliness was next to Godliness'. A clean home was a source of pride for many women and the expectation of most men – and not just in magazine advertisements. Such journals often carried articles on a regular basis about the cleaning of home interiors. For these and other reasons, therefore, most women did some cleaning every day, even if on Sunday it was only the cooker after the main meal.

WHAT A LIFE by GILBERT WILKINSON

" Farewell, my queen, it's work today for your little consort! "

From the *Daily Herald*, 3 June 1953.

When cleaning, housewives often wore a scarf tied around the head turban-style and a frilly apron or floral overall. The scarf could hide hair-curlers, as being seen with them, especially in public, was often viewed as socially degrading. Dusting would take place most days, although it might be sufficient to polish the furniture only once a week. Some people had woodblock or parquet floors, in which case floor polishing could take up a lot of time. Rugs and mats tended to predominate in most people's houses rather than fitted carpets, which only became a feature from the 1960s. Linoleum ('lino') was easier to keep clean but seen by some as a socially inferior form of floor covering. Floorboards might also be stained with varnish. Although electric polishers existed, most housewives used buckets and mops. Mansion polish was a well-known brand which in 1953 sold in tins for 10*d*, 1*s* 6*d* and 3*s* 9*d*. It polished floors, furniture and linoleum. Others continued to make their own polish from a mixture of paraffin and vinegar. Vacuum cleaners were already becoming popular, but most people still cleaned their mats weekly with a stiff brush.

Not every domestic task fell to women. Men were often willing to light fires, yet even this duty might fall to the housewife. It was quite a skill for anyone to place paper, wooden sticks and small pieces of coal in such a way that a fire would catch. If it didn't, then various stratagems were adopted, including blowing, fanning and holding up whole sheets of newspaper to encourage the fire to 'draw'. Nearby there might be a scuttle with coal to top up once the fire was under way or to bank it in should the occupants leave the house for a few hours and hope to return to a roaring fire and a warm room. In the morning the cinders might be sifted and some used again. The grate would also need cleaning.

Men might also do the washing up. Although dishwashers had been available in Britain since 1937, less than 1 per cent of households had one by this time. In 1948 Lever Brothers introduced Quix, the first liquid detergent designed specifically for washing up. Comprising 'concentrated suds', it cost 1*s* 3*d* and offered between two and three weeks' washing up. Sqeezy, the first plastic squeezable bottle, did not follow until 1956.

SEWING AND KNITTING

Although solid fuel was gradually being supplanted by gas or electric fires, few homes had central heating. Consequently the living room remained the focal point of the house and was where the family would gather, often around the radio set, radiogram or, especially after the coronation, the television. It might also be where sewing and knitting was done. Few housewives were without a sewing machine, although this was normally operated by a handle or a treadle. Electric models had existed since before the First World War, but their take-up was small – many preferred instead to purchase a small electric motor and convert an existing manual model.

Sewing machines were used for mending, dress-making and

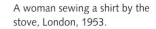

A woman sewing a shirt by the stove, London, 1953.

converting household linen into other items. Old blankets were made into cot covers; the best parts of tablecloths turned into tea, trolley or tray cloths; frayed towels given binding; sheets turned sides to middle and sewn back together again with as flat a seam as possible to avoid discomfort. Dylon, developed in the late 1940s, might be used to dye personal or household items. It cost 6*d* per tin and was available in many colours. White had been introduced in 1952 and navy blue, green and

pastels were the most popular colours of the time. Some women set aside a particular afternoon to sew; others with large families would in addition stitch, pick and darn – even nylon stockings. They would also make new clothes for themselves (a dress or skirt) or for others, such as shirts, trousers or swimsuits for children. Patterns were readily and cheaply available.

Patterns were also a feature of knitting. Women's magazines and wool manufacturers produced patterns cheaply and in abundance. The wool, usually obtained from specialist shops and department stores, would normally be sold in loosely coiled and twisted hanks known as skeins. These would be converted into balls before being used. Children were often involved in this process – one held the wool looped over outstretched hands while the other (or an adult) wound it into a ball. If no one was around to help, the skein could be stretched over two chairs placed back to back. In 1953 there was also equipment that would convert the wool into balls, and manufacturers had started offering wool in this form too.

RADIO

Radio was the most important source of information and entertainment in the home. Sometimes it was incorporated into a radiogram and regarded as a welcome and substantial piece of furniture. In contrast, there were radios that looked like vanity cases which switched on automatically when the lid was raised. Radio Rentals offered a model with pre-tuned selector switches which were colour coded.

In 1953, over 10 million sound-only licences were issued at £1 each. People often tuned into overseas radio stations in addition to the three BBC radio stations; newspapers provided details of broadcasts. Radio Luxembourg was particularly popular, offering light music that included a hit parade. Pete Murray was one of the station's presenters.

One BBC radio programme which had become essential listening for many people was *The Archers*. By 1953 this 'everyday story of country folk' was a popular and well-established radio programme. Its first trial episodes had been heard on the Midland Home Service in Whit Week 1950. It was first heard nationally on New Year's Day 1951 – at 11.45 a.m. The daily series was intended initially to last for three months. Within weeks it had secured a regular audience of 2 million, and an extended life. Furthermore *The Archers* was moved to the Light Programme's peak listening time of 6.45 p.m. This was its broadcast time in 1953 and the programme had an audience of over 8 million. So convincing a part of national life had *The Archers* become that listeners were sending in letters, birthday cards and Christmas greetings addressed to 'Brookfield Farm, Ambridge'. Similarly, there were topical inserts about the deaths of Queen Mary and Stalin.

Storylines in 1953 included Dan Archer being troubled by swine fever at the piggery, Tom Forrest mauled by a poacher and Walter Gabriel's sheep killed by dogs. In September the actor playing Gabriel (Robert Mawdesley) himself died. The part

Murphy A104 broadcast receiver, veneered in mahogany with gold plastic trim, *c.* 1949, offering improved sound quality.

went to Chris Gittins. But what seemed to arouse most concern and excitement was the love affair between Phil Archer and Grace Fairbrother. Coronation Eve found them roasting potatoes on the bonfire on Lakey Hill until four o'clock in the morning. It was then that she told him she would be spending a year in Ireland to train in horse management. Many listeners wondered whether she would return, or whether Phil, who had had romances with other girls in the area, would remain faithful. (They were to marry in the summer of 1955; Grace died the night ITV was launched.)

Mrs Dale's Diary was another established part of many people's lives. Mrs Dale being 'worried about Jim' was already becoming something of a catchphrase. The same could be said about some of the exchanges which featured in another programme of the time – *The Goon Show*. This had first been broadcast (under the title *Crazy People*) in May 1951. The term 'Goon' had been deliberately chosen. Although originally late-nineteenth-century slang from Boston, USA, meaning a simpleton, the word had a wider currency by the early 1950s. It had featured in the *Popeye* comic strip and was much used by British prisoners of war to describe their German guards. The stars in the 1953 series – Peter Sellers, Harry Secombe, Spike Milligan and Michael Bentine – thrived on nonsense; the title fitted the theme and purpose of the programme, with characters such as Major Bloodnok and Neddy Seagoon.

Take It From Here, written by Frank Muir and Dennis Norden and first broadcast in 1947, was extremely popular in 1953. It was a mix of variety and (in effect) serial revolving around the life of the Glum family. This comprised Mr Glum (Jimmy Edwards), his son the hopeless Ron (Dick Bentley) and Ron's long-suffering fiancée Eth (Joy Nichols). Another domestic comedy was *A Life of Bliss*. This was first broadcast in 1953 and concerned the day-dreaming bachelor David Bliss and the question of whether or not he would ever marry.

In preparation for Dr Alfred Kinsey's *Sexual Behaviour in the Human Female* an unidentified woman is interviewed by Dr Wardell B. Pomeroy, one of only four people who had access to Kinsey's reference files, 19 August 1953.

Another celebrated comic achieving even greater prominence in 1953 was Tony Hancock. He had already begun to make his name in various programmes, in particular as the tutor to ventriloquist Peter Brough's dummy in *Educating Archie*. This year saw him making regular appearances on *Forces All-Star Bill* and *Star-Bill – The Best in Britain's Showbusiness*. It was in May 1953 that the Goon Show producer suggested the format for what became *Hancock's Half Hour*, the first series of which began broadcasting in November 1954.

TELEVISION

In 1953 the BBC, with its one channel (405 lines), was the only provider of television in the country but, as a result of the spread of transmitters, could reach most of the nation. Televising the coronation gave the greatest single impetus to the purchase of television sets. In 1952 fewer than 1.5 million combined television and radio licences were issued. Almost 3.25 million were issued two years later. Such a licence cost £2 in 1953; a sound-only licence was £1. Television detector vans ensured that those households which needed a licence did indeed have one. The coronation broadcast, with over 20 million watching it for at least some part of the day, was the first programme to have had more viewers than listeners.

Although there were television programmes every day, broadcasting hours were relatively few, not continuous, and some programmes were in sound only. Much of daytime broadcasting was taken up by the testcard and a variety of accompanying music. Television aimed to please all sections of the population, however, and was gradually ceasing to be an essentially working-class form of entertainment.

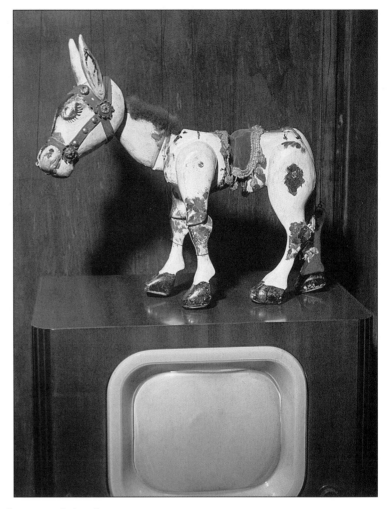

Muffin the Mule from the children's television programme of that name.

Television Newsreel, which had started in January 1948, was among the most popular programmes and was broadcast five times a week. It provided news of the nation and the world. *About Britain*, first broadcast in 1952, focused on national life. It typified the Corporation's attempt, in view of the growing audience outside the capital, to present programmes of interest to the nation as a whole. *Panorama* was launched in November 1953. Probably the most-discussed programme, however, was *What's My Line?* with Gilbert Harding. Variety was another staple of television at this time. Among those making their first appearance were Morecambe and Wise and Rolf Harris. The Children's Television Department had been set up in 1950 and *Watch with Mother* was broadcast from Monday to Friday from 3.45 to 4.00 p.m. Programmes featured included *Muffin the Mule* with Annette Mills, *Andy Pandy* and *The Flowerpot Men*; *Rag, Tag and Bobtail* was first televised on 10 September.

Growing Up in 1953 – Learning and Leisure

THE STRUCTURE OF EDUCATION

The structure of education in Britain was quite complex. Most pre-university education was through a mix of state and private (misleadingly known as 'public') schools. In 1953 education was free and compulsory for those aged between five and fifteen. The state sector was attended by over 90 per cent of children. In addition to primary (for those aged between five and eleven years) and secondary (eleven to fifteen), there was some nursery education (for the two- to five-year-olds). Furthermore, about 3 per cent of those in state schools were over fifteen, mostly because they intended to go on to university. Over 10 per cent of this age group were in the private school sector.

The school leaving age had been raised to fifteen under the 1944 ('Butler') Education Act. Under that legislation, pupils were to be given an education appropriate to their 'age, abilities and aptitudes'. But, in the absence of a national curriculum, it did not specify what this should be. The Act did ensure, however, that different forms of secondary education were available. These forms corresponded to and catered for the view that children's minds were of three types – abstract, mechanical and concrete. They resulted in the creation of the grammar, the secondary technical and secondary modern schools respectively. Together they formed what was known as the tripartite system. The grammar school was to provide society with the professions, the technical school the crafts and the secondary modern the less skilled and service sector, such as retailing.

Selection was by examination in the last year of primary school – the eleven plus. The exam was a series of 'general intelligence tests'. At this time it was generally believed that it was possible to measure intelligence independent of social or environmental factors. About a quarter of those who sat the eleven plus passed it, although the government preferred to argue that no one failed, as the purpose of the exam was to identify the most appropriate form of secondary education. The result (whatever it was) showed this. The child only 'failed' if sent to the wrong type of school.

The intention was that the grammar school should be for children who hoped to reach university and for others with an academic bias. Its curriculum was a mix of the humanities, languages (including Latin and possibly Ancient Greek) and sciences. Pupils at grammar school stayed on until at least sixteen, when they took the General Certificate of Education (GCE) at Ordinary ('O') Level. This was a single-subject examination which had been introduced in 1951 to replace the School Certificate, which represented study in a variety of subjects. David Hockney took his 'O' levels in 1953. He said that he had passed in English because he had provided the scenery for the Shakespeare play studied. When he sat the French paper he wrote on the script that he didn't know the language and drew pictures instead.

David Hockney.

There were also single-subject GCEs at Advanced ('A') and Scholarship ('S') Levels, which were taught in the sixth form and which had replaced the Higher School Certificate. Pupils sat six or more GCE 'O' Levels and two or three 'A' Levels. Few sat 'S' Levels and then normally only in one subject.

The secondary modern school provided a less demanding level of general education and with more of a practical bias. The curriculum was believed to be more closely related to the (perhaps presumed) interests, environment and ambitions of their pupils. The secondary technical school was the smallest of the three, with the education there more directly focused on the needs of industry. Where extant, it took those who had only just failed to make it to grammar school. Even so, such a policy reinforced the idea that a technical education was inferior to an academic one. In the state sector only grammar school pupils sat GCEs. In reality, however, it was expensive to provide all three types of secondary education and by the early 1950s

Local Education Authorities (LEAs) preferred to offer just grammar and secondary modern schools. Parents, too, preferred to see more grammar schools being built in their area as it increased the chance of their children securing a place.

However, this secondary school system was already under attack in 1953. Critics questioned how reliable the eleven plus was in identifying levels of ability and maintained that it decided not just the form of secondary education but invariably determined the nature of subsequent adult employment and lifestyle. There was little opportunity for redress or a second or later chance for those who did not make it to the grammar school. No exam or selectivity, but instead one single all-in (or 'comprehensive') school was one answer. Already by 1953 such a form of secondary education had been established in Windermere (1945) and Anglesey (1949); Kidbrooke, London's first purpose-built comprehensive school, was already under construction and opened in 1954.

LIFE IN STATE SCHOOLS

Generally speaking, primary education was mixed in both terms of gender and (though to a lesser extent) ability. Single-sex schools were, however, a feature of much secondary education and grammar schools in particular streamed according to ability. As required under the 1944 Education Act, there was a daily single act of worship which involved all the school. It was held in the school hall and was often known as 'assembly'. Religious instruction was also taught – the only compulsory subject in the school curriculum. Both were predominantly, if not entirely, Christian in outlook, although parents could withdraw their children if they wished.

Discipline and respect for teachers were both emphasised. Punishment for misdemeanours might take the form of 'lines' – writing out a single statement ('I must not talk in class') a certain number of times. This might also be known as 'an imposition'. Pupils could also be kept in after school hours or during the lunch break ('detention'). For the most serious of offences the cane could be used or, as a final resort, the miscreant might be expelled. Grammar schools had a prefect system drawn from members of the sixth form. They helped maintain discipline within the school, but outside the classroom, and could exact milder forms of punishment.

To enforce respect, in grammar schools at least, pupils would stand and collectively greet staff as they entered a classroom. Also staff would normally wear their university gowns. The academic nature of grammar school education was stressed, too, with greater emphasis than elsewhere on the setting and following up of

homework. Individual effort was encouraged through exams and the award of school prizes on Speech Day, which normally involved a guest with local or school links presenting the books and acknowledging the successes of the previous year. Parents would normally also attend this event. Corporate identity within the school was encouraged through loyalty to a House. This was particularly called upon for the annual sports day. Overall school identity was developed through the wearing of uniforms, a school song and inter-school competitions. These were not necessarily limited to sports events, as extra-curricular activities might include debating societies or quizzes. Hobby and interest clubs might also take place outside school hours.

Mealtime in a junior school in the early 1950s.

One-third of a pint of milk was available each day for children who wished to have it, although attitudes towards its consumption would vary according to the weather. The milk could be lukewarm and might 'go off' in summer, while it might be nearly frozen in the depths of winter. School dinners were equally not always welcome but they formed an important part of many children's lives. The meals were normally prepared at the school and the price was subsidised (remitted in cases of need). Nearly half of LEA pupils had school dinners at this time. There was also free transport for children who lived more than a reasonable distance from their school. This was normally interpreted as over two miles for those under eight and over three miles above that age. Many children enjoyed (and could safely undertake) the walk to school with their parent or friends while they might cycle or take a bus when older.

The school medical service conducted medical examinations and vaccinations as well as perhaps dental clinics and sun treatment for tuberculosis sufferers. It also investigated tendencies to rickets and growth disorders. There was also the nit nurse, who ruffled a child's hair and made grave pronouncements should anything be wrong. The medical room would display posters bestowing advice – in particular that 'coughs and sneezes spread diseases/trap them in your handkerchieves [sic]'.

ORGANISED LEISURE

There were numerous national voluntary youth organisations active in Britain at this time, focusing on the physical, mental and spiritual well-being of young people. The 1944 Education Act required LEAs to provide organised cultural and recreative leisure-time activities for children and young people. Therefore a partnership was established between the Ministry of Education, LEAs and voluntary organisations. Among the most significant at this time were the Girls' Friendly Society, Boy Scouts and Wolf Cubs, Girl Guides, Boys' Brigade, Young Men's (and Young Women's) Christian Association, National Association of Boys' Clubs and National Association of Mixed Clubs and Girls' Clubs (also known as Treasure Trove Holiday Club). There were also church clubs, settlement clubs (found in poorer urban areas) and special interest groups such as Young Farmers' Clubs (to encourage farming among schoolchildren), Red Cross and St John's Ambulance Brigade (first aid).

Together they offered a variety of activities and encouraged friendship, exercise, cultural and social activities which might, but did not necessarily, have a religious purpose. Clubs might have paid full-time youth leaders and a club room and might meet six nights a

week. Here there might be dances (with music from a radiogram), discussion groups and practical classes. Camping was popular with most children and young people, and gatherings could be on a very large scale. The first Indaba International Camp for Scouters had been held in 1952 in Gilwell Park, Epping Forest, Essex. That same year had seen an international camp for Girl Guides and one was to be held in 1954 for the Boys' Brigade to mark the centenary of the birth of its founder, Sir William Smith. Normally the summer camp would be on a smaller scale and involve sport, games, bathing and campfire songs. Boys' Brigade companies met during the week for drill, training and recreation; Sunday was for Bible Class. The Church Lads' Brigade, an Anglican organisation founded in 1891, offered boys a chance to play in a band (brass, bugle, flute or pipe), develop (tracking) skills and acquire 'the qualities of British and Christian manhood'.

The Young Women's Christian Association set up a Coronation Holidays and Travel Department to provide accommodation for those wishing to see the event. It also organised this year its first National Religious Drama Festival. The National Association of Boys' Clubs ran regional arts festivals which promoted drama,

Adventurous children testing the ice on Grantham Canal in 1953.

music and literature. It also offered a weekend course in London called *Adjustment to Industry* which was designed to develop 'the right attitude towards work and to show how industry fits into the whole life of the community'. The Girls' Friendly Society had a garden party in Lambeth Palace in coronation year and the Boys' Brigade gave a programme of physical training and light entertainment at the Royal Albert Hall in the presence of the Duke of Edinburgh.

GAMES AND TOYS

Daily school and perhaps membership of a Sunday school and/or organisation brought children into near continuous contact with each other and, given the high birth rate in the postwar years, the likely abundance of playmates and opportunities in the home, the street or park for games. Among the most popular were sport (especially football and cricket), hide and seek, skipping games and singing games which might involve an element of chase or elimination. Children might also have some kind of vehicle (most likely nailed together by an adult from used wood and old wheels) to give each other rides. Misdemeanours on the streets might include fighting, hitting balls into people's gardens, knocking and then running away from neighbours' doors.

The Annual Tri-ang Toy Fair. Susan Ellerker, aged eight, sits among the dolls.

Children had quite a wide variety of toys to choose from in 1953. Girls enjoyed playing with dolls and the linked delights of prams, dolls' houses and furniture. The clockwork (and increasingly electric) railway remained a favourite with boys. Tri-ang Railways as a name had been established in 1952. Such was its success that new premises were acquired the following year in Margate. Boys also played with soldiers, which might be made of wood, metal or plastic. There were also toys which might appeal to both genders, for example teddy bears, pedal motor cars and tricycles, roller skates, games, musical toys and puppets. Toy manufacturers, although strongly placed because of import restrictions, continued to innovate. Some pedal motor cars for instance had a shaft drive and a gear box giving two forward and reverse speeds as well as a neutral position. There were dolls with pliable vinyl heads and hair rooted into the scalp. Some dolls, to a limited extent, were able to walk automatically. Similarly some model vehicles now had fly-wheel drive instead of a clockwork mechanism. There was much excitement when, with a short push of the toy, it would continue for a while to run along on its own.

Children, partly inspired by comics and the mass media, knew they were living in a space age. There were already space rockets, space telephones and suits. Airfix's first aircraft construction kit – a Spitfire – appeared on the market at this time. Television had already started to influence children's choice of toys. Christmas 1953 saw particular interest in string-operated and glove puppets, especially in the form of Prudence the Kitten, Hank and above all Muffin the Mule. Film too was not without its impact. The success of *Ivanhoe* and *The Knights of the Round Table* meant that many children wanted model soldiers from these eras rather than the twentieth century. Children might also request a diecast Matchbox miniature coronation coach.

Those interested in sport might have received *Denis Compton's Annual*. Mainly a review of the cricket and football of the past year, the 1953 edition had six entries attributed to Compton, with such

'Picnic Time for Teddy Bears': the famous song came to life in Wells, Somerset, when two local sisters went exploring, November 1953.

1953 issue of the *Beano* comic.

features as 'My Cricket Gallery' (those featured included Colin Cowdrey, Tom Graveney, Jim Laker, David Sheppard and Fred Truman, who was cricketer of the year) and 'A chance for every boy' (to play cricket). Compton chose as his proudest day, however, being part of the Arsenal football team which had won the FA Cup in 1952.

COMICS

Although it had first appeared over seventy years earlier in January 1879, the now monthly *The Boy's Own Paper* (often known affectionately as the *BOP*) was still selling extremely well in 1953 both in Britain and some fifty other countries. Contributors at this time included W.E. Johns (with hero Biggles) and Hammond Innes. But in addition to adventure stories there were competitions, a letters page and regular features on such subjects as bicycle maintenance, photography, stamp collecting and other hobbies as well as sport and what a later generation would know as interviews with celebrities.

The *BOP* had been inspired by the Religious Tracts Society and maintained a strong moral outlook. The *Eagle* was similarly minded and, under its clergyman editor, sold a million copies a week. The adventures of Colonel Daniel MacGregor Dare and his associate Albert Digby in the spaceship *Ranger* continued to thrill. Enthusiasm for the comic and, to quote the advertisement of the time, 'a Christian philosophy of honesty and unselfishness', were channelled into an Eagle Club, whose members corresponded with the paper and on occasion met up. Other popular comics included *Girl*, *Swift*, *Lion*, *Tiger* (with 'Roy of the Rovers') and the *Beano*, whose Roger the Dodger and Minnie the Minx first appeared in 1953. *Topper*, the *Robin* (price 4d) and *TV Fun* (3d) were all launched this year.

A 1953 edition of the *Eagle*.

Concern remained over the content and popularity of American comics. These had become more widely known as a result of US servicemen reading and circulating them during the Second World War. A British market for them had begun to develop and such comics might be imported or, to save foreign exchange, printed in Britain. Anxiety centred around the violence, sex and racial hatred which seemed to predominate, along with graphic pictures or captions which were deemed to leave little to the imagination. A campaign against them was led by the National Council for the Defence of Children, and legislation was passed which sought to prevent the 'dissemination of certain pictorial publications' to those under fifteen.

SWEETS

For many children the first memorable event of 1953 took place on 4 February – the day sweets came off ration. To celebrate, the Edinburgh firm Duncan's distributed 8,000 pounds (weight) of sweets and chocolates to local schoolchildren. Not all places saw a significant increase in demand although children on the way to school often took advantage of buying their favourite sweets without being limited by points.

An advertisement for Spangles just before the end of sweet rationing.

Ice cream and iced lollies were popular too. The popularity of the iced lolly had increased in the postwar years because restrictions on dairy products had made ice cream less available. Flavours included aniseed, cough mixture, dandelion and burdock, lemon, liquorice, lime and, of course, orange. In 1953 the most popular iced lollies were Fluky Pops, Frupop, Lucky Koola and Topsy. A Topsy was given to each of the 32,000 children along the Embankment in London on Coronation Day. To deter litter, Topsy's makers offered children a coronation brooch for every six wrappers surrendered. There was also coronation rock. Back home, ice cream vans toured neighbourhoods, complete with chimes, although the Performing Rights Society argued that each van using music protected by copyright should pay 3 guineas. Consequently *Greensleeves* was used most.

Liquorice, Parma Violets and Love Hearts were in great demand. The last named were sweets with various messages and were a descendant of the Victorian 'conversation lozenges'. Some boys removed the wrapper and fixed the order of such sweets so as to determine who chose a particular message.

LIST OF SWEETS

Barratt's Sherbet Fountain (2*d*)
Devlin's Sports sweet cigarettes (2*d* for ten)
Dollar Film Star bubblegum (1*d* a strip, plus film-star photograph)
Mackintosh's Rolo (6*d*)
Flying Saucers
Razzle Dazzle chewing-gum balls
Blue Star Pure Sherbet Sucker, with liquorice tube (1*d*)
Big Chief Dream Pipe (liquorice) (1*d*)
Beat-all Lollies

CHRISTMAS

Although sweets and toys might feature throughout the year, especially at birthdays, they were above all an important – indeed for most children an essential – part of Christmas. Yet the preparations for and the celebrations of the festive season were also eagerly anticipated. There were few signs of the approach of Christmas before December, but thereafter each day brought new awareness and excitement. There would be school and Sunday school parties during this month, with children often encouraged to bring some food and drink just before or on the day. Depending on the children's age, such parties might take place during school hours or afterwards. The normally dour school hall would already be brightly decorated, the Christmas tree featuring prominently. The piano, so inextricably linked with assembly hymns or music lessons, would now provide the accompaniment for musical chairs or dancing (reluctantly practised in the previous weeks).

The armed services and some employers such as W.D. & H.O. Wills, the cigarette manufacturer, might also hold a children's party for their workforce. Such occasions might include food, games, a film show and be rounded off with a visit (and gift) from Father Christmas. The Ancient Order of Foresters in Epsom this year gave its first Christmas party for children since the war. Some 130 children were entertained by a ventriloquist and a puppet show. The celebrations ended with Father Christmas giving every child a present from the tree. Children in care and hospitals would also receive special attention in the build-up to as well as during the great day itself.

Children's enthusiasm for Christmas was perhaps best expressed in making their own home ready for the great occasion. Among the great delights were making paper chains from brightly coloured thin adhesive strips, cutting and sticking together 'something to hang on the tree' or putting up the lines of string which were to hang and display the Christmas cards so eagerly awaited. Manufactured decorations for room and Christmas tree were also readily available (particularly from Woolworths) and while electric tree (or 'fairy') lights were known, many still hung wax candles which, under suitable conditions, might be lit on occasion. A fairy or star normally crowned this favoured and natural feature of the time, likely to have been bought in the nearby market or shop.

Locally, too, children knew that Christmas was coming. By 1953 many towns had Christmas trees on public display and Father Christmas would appear at church bazaars or take up longer residence in local department stores. Perhaps found in a grotto, he might be assisted in the distribution of presents by elves or Uncle

Holly. The latter, created for Selfridges by Enid Blyton, had made his first appearance there in December 1949.

At last, 'T'was the night before Christmas', and young children waited expectantly for the hours to pass. As coal fires remained the single most popular form of domestic heating, it was readily accepted that Father Christmas could and would enter the home the traditional way, down the chimney (letters to him could, after all, be sent *up* the chimney though children remained anxious that they might be burnt or lost en route). Cocoa, perhaps in a Cadbury's 'Bournvita' light brown ceramic mug moulded into the form of a face, was popular with children at this time. In some households a sherry might be on offer, together with a mince pie for Santa and a carrot for the reindeer. These would be left on the mantelpiece; evidence that they had been consumed was looked for eagerly the following day.

For many children the great day itself involved emptying a Christmas stocking (with nuts, fruit and sweets) and unwrapping what had been brought by Father Christmas – even if it was six o'clock in the morning. Some parents might leave older children to enjoy some of the gifts while they attended Christmas Day Holy Communion or Mass, worshipping as a family later in the day. Other presents would be opened during the day. For the first Christmas since 1939 when sweets were no longer on ration, chocolate selection boxes of products manufactured by Cadbury's or Fry's were particularly popular. There were edibles, too, on the Christmas tree, including perhaps pink-and-white sugar mice.

A reduction in purchase tax (from 33⅓ per cent to 25 per cent) during the course of the year meant that toys were cheaper this Christmas. The continuing emphasis on toys for export and the aftermath of the increased demand for them at coronation street parties meant, however, that some toys (especially those made of metal) were in short supply, as manufacturers could not keep up with demand. Consequently home-made wooden toys – notably blackboards and forts – were popular gifts. Concern for less fortunate children was evident too: some 750 toys were sent by a Torquay Methodist Church to the Wandsworth Mission in London for distribution to poor families.

Fun in '53: Sport, Cinema and Holidays

FOOTBALL

Although less than its peak of forty-one million spectators (1948/49), the season attracted massive support, and the 1953 FA Cup was one of the most memorable to date. For many it was the sporting highlight of the year, which would be linked thereafter with the name of Stanley Matthews, who was born in February 1915 in Hanley, near Stoke-on-Trent, Staffordshire. The son of a hairdresser, Matthews showed that he had inherited his father's skill as a footballer when he was signed by Stoke City as an amateur player at fifteen and as a professional two years later. In the following season Matthews played sixteen times in the League side and the club was promoted to the first division. In September 1934 Matthews was awarded his first cap for England in a match against Wales. By the end of 1953 he had played for England thirty-eight times in full internationals and his skill as an outside right dribbler was renowned.

The FA Cup

Held on 2 May, the Coronation Cup Final was between Blackpool and Bolton Wanderers. Over 100,000 were at Wembley Stadium, many of them hoping that Stanley Matthews, playing for Blackpool and the first ever Footballer of the Year (1948), would take home a cup-winner's medal at last, having twice been on the losing side in recent years (1948 and 1951). Matthews himself realised that at thirty-eight this would be his last chance. The event was already notable as the Queen's first Cup Final and for the BBC's intention to cover the game in its entirety for the first time. Furthermore, for the first time League fixtures had been rearranged so as to avoid clashing with the Cup Final broadcasts: gates at other games on Cup Final day had been smaller in previous years. Through radio and television, this Cup Final had its biggest audience yet.

Stanley Matthews, the Blackpool outside right, demonstrates his wizardly skill as he steers the ball past Bolton's Barrass during the FA Cup Final at Wembley, 2 May 1953.

It was a beautiful day after nearly fifty hours of rain, with the ground a brilliant green. The Scots and Irish Guards appropriately played 'I'm a Lassie from Lancashire' and the stadium was full of rattles, ribbons, scarves, shirts and hats in tangerine or blue and white. Bolton scored after less than two minutes and were winning 3–1 within the first hour. It seemed all but over for Blackpool. But, with twenty-two minutes left, Stan Mortensen ('Morty'), who had scored in the first half, added a second. Bolton held out, however, until the last minute of normal time. But Jackie Mudie was brought down outside the box as he fastened on to another Matthews centre. Consequently Blackpool was awarded a free kick just outside the Bolton penalty area. Mortensen took the kick, aiming at the top corner of the net and scoring before the Bolton goalkeeper had time to move.

Extra time loomed and with it the prospect of a victory for Blackpool and Matthews. But in the final minute of injury time, Matthews demonstrated yet again why he was the 'Wizard of the Dribble'. Once more he headed towards the touchline and laid the ball back into the path of left-winger Perry, who swept it into the net from ten yards. From being 1–3 down at one stage, it was now 4–3! As Matthews later said, Blackpool had snatched victory from 'not just the jaws but the epiglottis of defeat'.

Matthews had his medal and the 1953 Cup Final has been associated with him ever since. Yet Matthews himself preferred to call it 'The Mortensen Final', this player being the first to score a hat-trick in a Wembley final. A lap of honour followed (another first) and Matthews was hoisted on to his team-mates' shoulders. He celebrated by knowingly drinking alcohol for the first time – champagne from the FA Cup itself. As each team had, unknown to

the other, booked the Café Royal for post-match celebrations, the sporting spirit between the two teams carried on through the evening. Blackpool's manager was Joe Smith, who had played for Bolton Wanderers when it had won the FA Cup in 1923 and 1926. Now he had a further victory. Referring to Matthews's and Mortensen's role in the game he declared, 'Cometh the hour, cometh the Stan – and I had two of them.' For Matthews it was only when it was all over that, speaking aloud to himself, he could rightly claim 'I've done it at last.'

Outside Blackpool Town Hall: Stanley Matthews and Harry Johnston return home parading the FA Cup, 5 May 1953.

Other Football Fixtures

Meanwhile amateur club Walthamstow Avenue could only look on with regret. They had beaten two league clubs (Watford and Stockport County) earlier in the contest and went on to hold Manchester United to a 1–1 draw at Old Trafford in the fourth round. They lost the replay 5–2 at Highbury.

Wembley was also the scene of shock: it was on 25 November 1953 that England lost its first ever match against a team from outside the British Isles – Hungary. The Hungarians' victory was watched from the royal box by Jimmy Hogan, a Lancastrian and guest of the winning side. He had been interned in Budapest in the First World War and subsequently became that country's national coach. His contribution to developing an impressive side had not been forgotten. England's captain was Billy Wright and other players included Stanley Matthews, Stan Mortensen and Jackie Sewell, whose £34,000 transfer from Notts County to Sheffield Wednesday had broken the record.

Hungary scored in the opening minutes, but Sewell soon equalised. Even so it was 4–2 at half-time. The Hungarian side scored twice more in the second half, England once with a goal by Alf Ramsay. The 6–3 result was a suitable revenge for the 6–2 defeat which the Hungarians had suffered on their last visit to London in 1936. The team's return by train through Hungary was met everywhere with flowers and gifts. Six months later England played them again, this time in Budapest – losing 7–1.

Earlier in the year, during an overseas tour, England had drawn 0–0 in a match against Argentina (rain had stopped play after 23 minutes) but had beaten Chile 2–1 and the USA 6–3, the latter game before a very small crowd in New York. This was a welcome victory given that England during its first appearance in the World Cup (1950) had been beaten 1–0 when playing a part-time team representing the USA.

Arsenal, captained by Joe Mercer, was top of Division 1, but only after a very close last match of the season against Burnley, who took the lead in the third minute. Fortunately for the Gunners, Alex Forbes equalised with his only goal of the season, while Lishman and Logie added to the score. Arsenal won 3–2 and the title, a record seventh, was theirs only because of goal average. They and Preston had identical results – some twenty-one wins, twelve draws and nine defeats – but the goal average was 1.51 to North End's 1.41. Manchester United, that year's holders of the Football League championship, finished eighth.

The other champions were Sheffield United (Division 2), Bristol Rovers (Division 3 South) and Oldham Athletic (Division 3 North). The top scorer was Charlie Wayman (Preston North End) with 24 goals and Nat Lofthouse (Bolton Wanderers) was 1953's Footballer of the Year. Among his achievements was 6 goals against the League of Ireland at Molineux on 24 September 1952. This was a record for an Inter-League match.

In Scotland, 1953 was Rangers' year. This team and Stirling Albion headed the Scottish League Divisions A and B respectively.

The Scottish FA Cup Final was between Rangers and Aberdeen. It ended in a draw; Rangers won the replay 1–0. Such victories added to the string of successes under Willie Struth, by then in his 75th year and manager since 1920. During that time the team had won the Championship eighteen times, ten FA Cups and three League Cups. A former stonemason and a professional runner, he had had little experience as a player before being appointed trainer. He became manager when the previous boss at Ibrox Park died in an accident.

Derek Dooley

On a sadder note, the career of Derek Dooley, Sheffield Wednesday's centre-forward, came to a sudden end. He broke his right leg while playing against Preston in February. Dooley was treated for a double fracture at Preston Royal Infirmary and was about to be discharged when it was discovered that gangrene had set in and his condition became critical. As a result he had to have his right leg amputated. There was genuine widespread sorrow at the way a promising career in football was now over. At this time a Mr Coulton, an insurance clerk, won the first dividend on both Littlewoods and Vernons Treble Chance. On being presented with a cheque for £109,000 by Sally Ann Howes, he said he would send £3,000 to the disabled player. Dooley, however, continued to be involved in football in Sheffield and was awarded the MBE for services to sport in the New Year's Honours for 2003.

CRICKET: ENGLAND WINS THE ASHES

The Australian touring team was led by Lindsay Hassett, who had toured England before and now succeeded Donald Bradman as captain. In this, his last series against England, he headed the batting with 365 runs. Indeed, taken as a whole, when he retired later in the year only Bradman among Australians had made more runs. Len Hutton captained England.

The first Test Match was held at Trent Bridge, Nottingham. Alec Bedser took 14 wickets and in so doing passed Sydney Barnes's record of 189 wickets for England. Barnes, whose first-class cricket career had begun in 1894, was there to congratulate him. Rain curtailed play and the test ended in a draw. The weather was better for the second test, which was held at Lord's. In the first innings, Australia was all out for 346; England for 372. The high point was the last day. In its second innings Australia had made 368 while England had lost Hutton, Graveney and Kenyon for 12 runs and at 73

runs, Compton, the Brylcreem Boy, was out for 33. This brought Trevor Bailey and Willie Watson together for the next four hours. They put on 163 for the fifth wicket and saved England. Nearly 138,000 watched this test – an average of 27,000 a day, with people sitting on the grass. The gates were closed to a further 10,000. The third test again suffered from bad weather. In the final hour of the fifth day Australia lost 8 wickets for 35 but the result was another draw, as was the fourth test.

The fifth and final test, played at the Oval, was to be the climax. After the first innings, England was set 132 runs to win. Under these favourable circumstances, Hassett gave himself one over and then

brought on Arthur Morris. Edrich and Compton had put on 39 together, and just 5 runs were needed for victory. Edrich scored a single and Compton made one of his famous sweeps off Morris's fourth ball. The crowd rushed forward, thinking it was all over. But Alan Davidson at backward short leg stopped the ball and the crowds, somewhat frustratedly, made their way back behind the boundary line. Morris bowled again and Compton swept it past all opposition – *this* time it could only be a 4. The crowd's response was such that if the ball did reach the boundary, it certainly was never seen again. Edrich and Compton squeezed their way back through the exuberant crowd. England had regained the Ashes after twenty years.

A panoramic view of the scene at the Oval as the crowd celebrates England winning the Ashes series against Australia, 19 August 1953.

A crowd outside a radio shop in High Holborn listening to the broadcast of the final test between England and Australia at the Oval.

Len Hutton acknowledges the cheers of the crowd acclaiming England's victory against Australia.

HORSE-RACING

The victorious England cricket team, August 1953.

This was a memorable year for Gordon Richards. Champion jockey yet again (since 1925 he had been awarded that title twenty-six times), he secured a win that had long eluded him. Just a few days after the Coronation Honours, when he became the first jockey to be knighted, he won the Derby at his twenty-eighth attempt. Some twenty-seven horses were at the starting post and included the Queen's horse Aureole. Bred at the royal stud, Sandringham, his trainer was Captain Cecil Boyd-Rochfort and his rider Harry Carr. Aureole had won the Lingfield Derby, so his prospects for the Derby were good. In contrast, Richards's horse, Pinza, owned by Sir Victor Sassoon, was rather large and thought less likely to win. However, he won by four lengths and later in 1953 also succeeded in winning the King George VI and Queen Elizabeth Stakes at Ascot; Pinza was again second. Richards's first Derby success was also to be his last. He was injured in 1954 when a horse fell on him in a paddock; as a result he retired from racing that year, becoming a successful trainer instead. Pinza too had retired by then. The Coronation Cup was won by the five-year-old Zucchero, which had been trained by Payne and ridden by Lester Piggott.

GOLF

The British narrowly missed winning the Ryder Cup. Daly and Bradshaw won Britain's only foursome point and each won his single. The outcome rested on Alliss and Hunt, the youngest players in the match. In a very exciting finish, each took six on the last hole when two fives would have won the match for Britain – the final result being 5½–6½.

Perhaps the most memorable golfing event of the year, however, was the Open Championship at Carnoustie and the presence for the first and only time of the American Ben Hogan. The US Professional Golfers' Association champion in 1946 and 1948, it looked as though his career was over one foggy morning in

Sam Snead, the American golfer, drives off from the first tee in a foursomes match during the two day Ryder Cup tournament at Wentworth. With his team captain Lloyd Mangrum he was opposing Britain's Eric Brown and John Panton, 2 October 1953.

February 1949. As he returned from the Phoenix Open with his wife, a Greyhound bus emerged from the fog and came towards them head-on. Hogan flung himself across his wife to protect her and in so doing saved himself as well. In the impact, the steering wheel was forced through the driver's seat. Even so, Hogan suffered major injuries and it was thought unlikely that he would ever play golf again. But his determination and skill were such that his record in major championships over the following four years represents the greatest sequence in golf history. His recovery also inspired the Hollywood film *Follow the Sun*, which had been made in 1951 and starred Glenn Ford.

Hogan prepared thoroughly for the British Open. He had to learn to deal with a green which he found woolly and slow, as well as with the British golf ball which was smaller than the American version. He needed to play two qualifying rounds: huge crowds gathered to watch him and a northbound train halted on the nearby track to enable everyone to see Hogan's first competitive stroke in Scotland. Afterwards, as was now always the case, he needed to bathe his legs in Epsom salts. On the first day of the championship he shot a seventy-three, three strokes off the lead. Among the crowd watching him was Frank Sinatra, who was performing in Dundee. On the last day two rounds were to be played and Hogan had no time to bathe his legs. He suffered excruciating pain, already had a cold and a temperature of 103 degrees. He almost matched the course record on the first round and did so on the second – to take the championship by four strokes.

JIM PETERS, MARATHON MAN

On 13 June an optician from Mitcham, Surrey, established a new world record in one of the most demanding of sporting events. Jim Peters ran the marathon from Windsor Castle to Chiswick in 2 hours, 18 minutes and 40.2 seconds. This was 2 minutes faster than his performance at the 1952 Helsinki Olympics (where he was beaten by Emil Zatopek) and 10 seconds faster than the then current world record held by the Japanese runner Yamada. Peters attributed his success to his training – running an average of 100 miles a week in the intervening period – and to a slower pace in the earlier stages of the race, enabling him to make a spectacular finish.

CINEMA

Going to the pictures remained a popular though diminishing leisure-time activity. Postwar audiences had peaked in 1946, when it

THE CRUEL SEA is cruel but never cheats the heart, says PAUL HOLT

This is Britain's best war film

By Paul Holt

THE best British war film done in peacetime is "The Cruel Sea," opening at the Leicester Square Theatre on Friday.

It is bold, honest, does not tug unfairly at the emotions, does not cheat the heart.

Like great poetry, it is beauty remembered in tranquillity. This is the beauty of courage.

The film, taken from the famous novel by Nicholas Monsarrat, tells the story of the Battle of the Atlantic.

There are no false heroics, nor false heroes.

The only man in the cast you are likely to recognise is Jack Hawkins, who plays the Commander of the Compass Rose, a corvette on convoy duty.

He does so splendidly in his task to build up the character of a stern, lonely, devoted sea captain that the future must be rosy for him.

Jack Hawkins and Virginia McKenna in *The Cruel Sea*. From the *Daily Herald*, 25 March 1953.

was estimated that about one-third of the British population went to the cinema at least once a week. Cinema was, however, most popular among the under-thirties. Many children still went to the pictures on Saturday morning while women at home might attend a matinee, perhaps combining it with afternoon tea nearby or in another part of the cinema.

Programmes, normally comprising two films, trailers for forthcoming pictures and a newsreel, were often continuous. People arrived and left mid-performance, nudging any companion when about to depart with the words 'This is where we came in'. Sometimes cinemas might temporarily abandon this policy. The Scala at St Ives, Cornwall, did so when *Limelight*, made in 1952 and starring Charlie Chaplin, came to the town in April 1953. The performance would close with the playing of the National Anthem. While some would rise, others would leave quickly, perhaps because they had a particular tram or bus to catch.

The State continued to support the British film industry, operating a quota system which guaranteed British output at least 30 per cent of screen time for long films and 25 per cent for short films. The three groups originated by the National Film Finance Corporation (which included Pinewood and Elstree), together with London Films and Ealing Studios, produced most of the British feature films at this time. Denham Studios had undergone rapid contraction since the late 1940s and was auctioned off in March.

The major British film productions of the year included *Trouble in Store*, *The Titfield Thunderbolt*, *Moulin Rouge* and *The Cruel Sea*. Norman Wisdom's first film, in which he played a hapless shop-window dresser, *Trouble in Store*, was so well received at its first showing towards the end of 1953 that it held no première but went on general release immediately. His song ('Don't Laugh at Me') reached the top ten in early 1954. An Ealing comedy, *The Titfield Thunderbolt*, concerns a village's response when its railway branch line is threatened with closure. It starred Stanley Holloway and John Gregson. *Moulin Rouge*, written and directed by John Huston, was a fictional film biography of the French artist Toulouse Lautrec and effectively evoked late nineteenth-century Paris. It starred the US actor Jose Ferrer, whose legs were often bound up painfully at the knee to portray the short stature of the artist. The theme music became a major hit during the year. *The Cruel Sea* was based on Nicholas Monsarrat's bestselling novel, and was itself a huge box-office success. Its subject was life and death on an Atlantic corvette during the Second World War. It starred Jack Hawkins (as Lieutenant Commander Erickson), Donald Sinden, Stanley Baker, Denholm Elliott, Virginia McKenna and Moira Lister. At the time this film was being planned, there were no corvettes in the Royal Navy. Ealing Studio, however, acquired one on its return from being loaned to Greece, before being broken up. Most of the filming was done in the Plymouth area. The impression of sailing in the North Sea in mid-winter was achieved using plaster icicles, ice and frost, together with heavy clothing. The shooting took place in brilliant summer weather, watched by hundreds of more suitably clad people on yachts and pleasure boats. Monsarrat, delighted by the film adaptation, sent Hawkins a copy of *The Cruel Sea* inscribed 'To Lieutenant Commander Erickson masquerading as Mr Hawkins'.

Charlie Chaplin at Lambeth town hall, having handed over a cheque 'for the poor of Lambeth', 1953. (© *Lambeth Archives*)

However, the British Film Academy voted *Genevieve* the best film of the year. It was a comedy in which two couples who are veteran car enthusiasts engage in friendly rivalry in a race on the way back from the annual London to Brighton car rally. 'Genevieve' is the name of the car owned by one couple, played by John Gregson and Dinah Sheridan; Kenneth More and Kay Kendall are the rivals. The film could have made Kay Kendall a major star, but she died a few years later of leukaemia. Larry Adler wrote and played the film music, but was only credited with this on the British version. The American print substituted Muir Mathieson, who also received the Oscar nomination. This was because Adler was blacklisted in the USA at the time.

Hollywood, increasingly aware of (and anxious about) the impact of television causing loss of audiences, hoped to increase attendances with new forms of film-making and stereophonic sound. *The House of Wax* was the first major three-dimensional (3-D) film. The action takes place in a New York wax museum run by Matthew Burke (played by Roy Roberts) and his sinister partner Professor

Ah! **Kensitas –**
that's Good!

From washing up most husbands shrink.
They say they won't go near the sink.
But oh! they will... if wives but think
Of Kensitas – that's good!

(Kensitas – the fresher, smoother cigarette)

"Kensitas –
that's Good!"

OUR BELIEF THE FINEST LEAF

Kensitas
CIGARETTES
Extra Size

20 Kensitas 20

It's the ripe mellow tobacco in Kensitas
that gives real smoking pleasure

OUR BELIEF, THE FINEST LEAF... *KENSITAS—THAT'S GOOD!*

Jarrod (Vincent Price). There are various camera tricks, including chairs appearing to be thrown into the audience and villains jumping out of the screen. Ironically André de Toth, the Hungarian-American director, only had one eye and was unable to experience the effect.

Another response was CinemaScope, the wide-screen process copyrighted by Fox in 1953. It involved a slightly curved screen two and a half times the normal size and gave the impression of a three-dimensional picture. It was first used in *The Robe*. A biblical best-seller, the film told how the followers and opponents of Jesus are affected by the robe stripped from Him at the time of the Crucifixion. Directed by Henry Koster, Richard Burton was the lead star, playing the part of Marcellus, the Roman officer who was in charge of the execution of Christ.

Feeling guilty thereafter, he is converted to Christianity and chooses to die for his new religion. Jean Simmons plays the woman who first misunderstands him and finally falls in love with him. Victor Mature led Marcellus to the new faith – a role intended originally intended for Burt Lancaster. The film was a great success in America and the UK, where the British Board of Film Censors unusually permitted the figure of Christ to be portrayed. Unfortunately, though, on a subsequent return to his Welsh home a neighbour's five-year-old child refused to play football with Burton as he had 'crucified Christ'. Even so, as Burton himself was to admit, *The Robe* brought him 'more money than he thought there was in the world'.

Burt Lancaster may have lost out on *The Robe* but did well in another US production seen by cinema-goers in 1953. He had a leading role (as Sergeant Milton Warden) in *From Here to Eternity*, which included the steamy affair with Karen Holmes. This part, originally offered to Joan Crawford, was played by Deborah Kerr. The film itself was awarded eight Oscars – the highest number for any single film since *Gone with the Wind* (1939).

Other American films which did well in Britain included *Calamity Jane* (with Doris Day), *How to Marry a Millionaire* (Betty Grable, Marilyn Monroe and Lauren Bacall), *Roman Holiday* (Gregory Peck and Audrey Hepburn) and *Shane*, in which the title role was played to excellent effect by Alan Ladd. It had five Oscar nominations, including Best Film (which was won by *From Here to Eternity*), but

Graham Greene receiving a literary award in 1952: the film of his novel *The Third Man* was a great US success in 1953.

only took home that for cinematography. British films which did well in America during the year included *Hamlet*, *The Red Shoes*, *The Third Man*, *The Lavender Hill Mob* and *The Man in the White Suit*. There was no premier award this year at the Venice Film Festival. Instead, three films shared second place, including *Moulin Rouge*.

HOLIDAYS

For many people in paid work, Sunday was the only complete day off. In addition to that weekly break, there were six statutory public (and paid) holidays in England and Wales (two each at Christmas and Easter), Whit Monday (which was seven weeks after Easter and normally in May) and the first Monday in August. In addition most employees had at least one week's holiday with pay and many had at least two. Often, however, the timing of the holiday would be determined by the employer. In the north there were 'Wakes weeks' (the traditional northern factory-town holidays) in mid-summer; in Swindon the railway works (still the largest single employer) closed for the first two weeks of July, which meant that the school holidays also began at that time and those employed elsewhere in the town might also have their holidays then.

Certainly this holiday break in Swindon (known as 'Trip' fortnight) was headline news for the local paper in the run-up to and aftermath of the great get-away of some 8,000 people on the Friday

Butlin's THE IDEAL FAMILY HOLIDAY

A real holiday together by the sea is every family's greatest joy, finest benefit — and foremost problem. For where in the world can everyone from baby upwards be free to enjoy themselves without all the worries of entertainment, constant supervision and rainy-day boredom?

The answer, in one word, is Butlin's — those wonderful Holiday Camps which make a special point of providing the best of all family holidays. For health and happiness — bring your family to Butlin's this summer.

FREE BROCHURE : Send postcard to :—
BUTLIN'S LTD., (Dept. H.B.) 439 OXFORD STREET, LONDON, W.1

and Saturday. There were extra late-night buses on the Friday to enable people to catch special trains from around 10 p.m. to St Ives, Newquay, Blackpool or, at just before midnight, Penzance. Extra buses and taxis were also operating from before five o'clock the following morning. The first train to Paignton was at 6 a.m. and the near 7,000 people to this and other seaside destinations were seen off by the acting station master, the works manager and other senior railway staff. People here as elsewhere often went on holiday with others and returned to the same resort year after year. The largest group on this occasion consisted of seven families (some twenty-six people) spending the next week together in chalets and caravans in Aberystwyth. They had done this since the First World War.

Local seaside resorts remained popular destinations. But many were prepared to travel further afield. Publicity offices of seaside towns had issued brochures for some time, but these now often included colour photographs. A small (but increasing) number were going on package holidays abroad, although there was a limit on how much money might be taken out of the country. Cook's tours continued to delight. In 1953 the state-owned company offered a seven-day trip to Bruges, Antwerp, Brussels, Paris and Versailles for 25 guineas. A twelve-day visit to the French and Italian Riviera cost 49 guineas.

However, the seaside remained the most popular destination, whether for a 'day out', a holiday weekend or the main summer break. Similarly, public transport was still heavily used. During Easter, British Railways ran additional trains to the West Country (especially from the capital) and over 3,000 extra buses left Victoria coach station. But car ownership was growing rapidly (though driving lessons could cost 15s per hour) and branded petrol had been reintroduced in February, having been absent since the start of the war. Premium grades were expensive but gave more miles per gallon.

Enjoying the Seaside

Easter 1953 was the first opportunity for people to enjoy a short break. Crowds in Torquay were described at being 'almost of summer density'. Police took control of several pedestrian crossings to regulate the streams of cars and people. Paignton Zoo had a particularly high number of visitors. Similarly, the August Bank Holiday attracted a great many long-distance visitors. A sea-front restaurant in Torquay offered breakfast from 3 a.m. and trippers who left Lancashire and the Midlands in the early hours cooked breakfast on the beach at Llandudno. One couple who had travelled to Devon from Liverpool for this weekend had discovered on arrival late at night that they had left the address of where they were

THE NEW BOND (Mark 'C') MINICAR
has arrived !

★ **£280 !**
★ **85 M.P.G.!!**
★ **50 M.P.H.!!!**
★ **£5 TAX!!!!**

DEMONSTRATIONS AND ADVICE, etc.
FROM THE DISTRIBUTORS FOR THIS AREA

SEYMOUR HORWELL GARAGES
Courtenay Street   **(Tel. 545)**   **Newton Abbot**

Advertisement from the *Herald Express*, 16 April 1953.

Terry towelling for the beach

A new colourful jacket for the beach—made of terry towelling. It has a zip-fastener down the front.

Advertisement from the *Evening Standard*, 16 June 1953.

staying at home. They phoned a friend, asking them to break into their home and find the details. Understandably they informed the police before embarking on the raid. Overnight accommodation was not a problem for some visitors to Brighton – they slept on the beach and had a pre-breakfast swim.

Westcliff-on-Sea Remembered

In early August a whirlwind alarmed hundreds of people on the beach and esplanade of this Essex resort. A slight breeze blowing off the cliffs suddenly became a gale involving a stretch of about a hundred yards. The wind blew holidaymakers off the esplanade; deck chairs and clothing were blown into the sea. There was a 60-foot-high water spout near the shore. The wind lifted one middle-aged visitor from the sea wall into the water. She received treatment for head injuries. A further dozen required first aid for cuts and bruises. The whole incident lasted about six seconds. Once the wind subsided bathers swam and retrieved floating deck chairs and clothing.

The World Beyond the Shores

BRITISH EMPIRE AND COMMONWEALTH

The term 'British Empire' was still used at this time, although it was often coupled with another phrase, namely 'The (British) Commonwealth of Nations'. Commonwealth members and Empire territories were to be found throughout all five continents. The Dominions, each with their own Governor-General appointed by the monarch, in 1953 comprised Ceylon, Pakistan, the Union of South Africa, Canada, New Zealand and the Commonwealth of Australia. India was the only republic at the start of the year, but was soon to be joined by Pakistan. Within the Empire itself there were colonies, some of which were self-governing, protectorates, mandates and a condominium.

The Colonies

Although India, 'the jewel in the crown', had been independent since 1947, the government was able to represent the transformation of Empire into Commonwealth as a success. It was argued that the process was a triumph of British statesmanship and that there was a long-established programme of preparing dependent states for self-government. Even so, the prevailing, bipartisan political sentiment in 1953 was that Britain's African Empire would probably continue until the end of the twentieth century. Economic development and constitutional changes were deemed necessary before control could be relinquished over these territories. The major legislative achievement here was the Rhodesia and Nyasaland Federation Act. This grouped the areas concerned to create the Central African Federation. It was argued that such integration would create a prosperous dominion which would attract investment for both private industry and public projects, such as the construction of the Kariba Dam on the Zambezi River. The protectorate of Northern Rhodesia was, for instance, one of the world's chief producers of copper, while Southern Rhodesia had a thriving economy. Nyasaland was the third territory in the proposed federation and was included primarily for geographical convenience. But the federation's constitutional arrangements were complex; in particular, Southern Rhodesia retained the self-governing status it had enjoyed since 1923 while the other two areas remained the responsibility of the Colonial Office.

But if in London gradualism was believed to be the key for the future of the African colonies, there were those in the territories themselves who sought to be rid of white settlers and control as soon as possible and pursued policies to achieve this. In 1953 this was most evident in Kenya.

Kenya

Kenya had been formed in 1920 from the East African Protectorate. The Kikuyu, the most powerful group of people in the vicinity of the capital, Nairobi, formed a political organisation known as the Kikuyu Central Association, which campaigned for, among other things, the restoration of land which they claimed had been unfairly taken from them by the Europeans. In 1929 a young representative of the Association, Jomo Kenyatta, was sent to London to pursue the case and make contact with sympathetic Labour MPs. He was to be away from Kenya for most of the next seventeen years, making a living as a journalist, farmer – and as an extra in *Sanders of the River*.

By 1940 the Kikuyu people had emerged as the leaders of African resistance to white settler supremacy and, in effect, British rule.

The caption from the *Evening Standard*, 16 June 1953, reads: The sun shines over London as the *Kenya Castle* docks, but for Mrs Josephine Marlow (left) it can never compare to the sun over Solwezi. Next to her is Mrs Heather White. Would she ever return to trouble-spot Kenya? Certainly! Thelma Adams (third from left) is sad to be back . . . the social life was 'terrific'. Mrs Douglas Paterson, extreme right, who found romance in South Africa, returns in September.

Kenyatta leaves court in handcuffs during his trial, 5 December 1952.

The Association was banned and its leaders in Kenya imprisoned. Kenyatta returned to Kenya in 1946 as something of a national hero and soon became a leader in the Kenyan African Union, which campaigned for greater indigenous political participation in the colony. Also in 1946 a secret Kikuyu society known as the Mau Mau began to operate. It was anti-European, anti-government and anti-Christian. By restoring ancient customs of oath-taking and murder, it aimed to drive white farmers and their labourers out of the traditional Kikuyu lands.

The Mau Mau revolt broke out in May 1952, with attacks on property and, by October, the murder of some fifty-nine anti-Mau Mau Africans. A new governor, Sir Evelyn Baring, arrived in September and declared a state of emergency the following month. The Kenya regiment and police reserves were mobilised and Home Guards formed. The Kenyan African Union was believed to be behind the Mau Mau, and Kenyatta, along with other leaders, was arrested. The organisation was banned, more radical leaders took over and terrorism became more widespread. Europeans were attacked and killed for the first time at the end of October. Some 3,500 Kikuyu squatters were moved off European farms into the reserves and by the end of November 1952, 13,000 Kikuyu had been detained, of whom 2,000 were later released and 5,000 charged. In January 1953 the Ruck family – a husband and wife and their young son – were hacked to death with pangas (bush knives) by the Mau Mau. Settler outrage increased further.

Kenyatta was put on trial before the end of the year because of his links with the Mau Mau, including the administration of its oaths. By in effect bribing the presiding judge (an *ex gratia* payment ten times his annual salary was made together with removal expenses to leave Kenya afterwards) and securing perjured evidence from the chief prosecution witness, the authorities obtained a conviction and Kenyatta was imprisoned. After his conviction in early 1953, police proceeded with mass arrests. On 22 March, 2,500 were detained after a police raid in Nairobi and the following day a further 3,500 people twenty-five miles away at Thika. In all some 80,000 Kikuyu, about 30 per cent of this ethnic group's male members, were eventually placed in detention.

On 26 March 1953 the Lari massacre occurred, which attracted considerable attention. Lari, a Kikuyu village, at Uplands, some forty miles north-west of Nairobi, was destroyed and over seventy men, women and children killed with a further fifty missing, presumed dead. The attack was launched in bright moonlight, involving a force of between 300 and 500 Mau Mau. Simultaneously lorries loaded with about sixty fighters drove into a police station twenty miles away, killed a policeman and police informer and seized weapons, together with boxes of ammunition. Those held in the cells were released.

The attacks that night around Lari witnessed, according to one report, 'gangs slaughtering all they met in a seven-mile strip of the Uplands area', with families burned alive in their wooden dwellings or murdered as they fled them. Shortly afterwards the police raided an African residential area in Nairobi and interrogated 15,000 people, of whom over 1,000 were detained. Special courts were also established in the Uplands area.

The administration in Nairobi continued to take action, with troops brought from Britain to support local forces and police. Officers of the colonial service were loaned from neighbouring colonies, and East Africa was made a separate military command directly under the War Office. The military measures taken led many Mau Mau members to withdraw into the Aberdare mountains. Similarly, aerial bombing and the denial of food caused others to leave the forests for Mount Kenya. Detaining Kikuyu in reserves led to labour shortages for European farmers, overcrowding and food shortages on the sites as well as the spread of Mau Mau ideas by activists affected by this policy.

In October 1953 General Sir George Erskine, Commander-in-Chief, East Africa, said that although the fight against the terrorists looked 'much better', there was no military answer to the situation in Kenya. The problem was purely political. Kenyatta

remained in prison until April 1959. He became Prime Minister of self-governing Kenya in 1963 and its President on independence the following year.

Nairobi: an elderly Kikuyu and his wife, parents of a juvenile offender, being visited by an African probation officer.

EARTHQUAKES IN GREECE AND CYPRUS

In early August a series of earthquakes, worse than those which had destroyed Corinth in 1928, affected islands in the Ionian Sea. That in Cephalonia killed one hundred people and injured more than twice that number. Two villages (Sami and Aghia Efthimia) and others along the Peloponnese west coast were destroyed. The Port of Vathy, the capital of Ithaca, was hit by tidal waves and the tremors were felt as far away as Athens. A British destroyer sailed from Malta with supplies, and the Queen sent a message of sympathy to the King of Greece. The United States provided helicopters which had been taking part in joint naval exercises with the Royal Navy off Malta.

In all, over 120 earthquake shocks were registered in five days. Eye-witnesses compared the damage with the effects of the atomic bomb on Hiroshima and spoke of islands appearing to sink under the boiling seas. Reports from the Greek Navy told how mothers searched in the darkness for the bodies of their children lying under the piles of debris and, not finding them, tried to kill themselves. Rescue and relief operations were coordinated on warships anchored off Argostoli, the destroyed capital of Cephalonia.

About a month later an earthquake hit south-west Cyprus in the Paphos district of the island. It destroyed the villages of Stroumbi and Kithasi, killing forty and making some 1,500 people homeless. Limassol, which had experienced an earth tremor the previous year, suffered damage yet again. There was only one fatality – a seven-month-old baby – but many in the nearby villages were injured.

THE KOREAN WAR

The People's Democratic Republic of Korea (North Korea) invaded the Republic of Korea (South Korea) on 25 June 1950, capturing Seoul a few days later. The South front line had stabilised in November 1951. By January 1953 the war had been going on for over two and a half years, and the Republic of Korea was now supported in its efforts to defeat the North, which was backed by the People's Republic of China, by sixteen (of sixty) members of the United Nations. These included Britain, Canada and the USA. Five nations provided medical assistance to the UN command and forty-six nations offered it economic assistance.

North Korea's Commander-in-Chief was its Prime Minister, Marshal Kim; the forces for the South were under the UN. The 'unified command' in 1953 was under the American general, Mark Clark. Truce talks, which had begun in July 1951 between the United Nations and North Korea, had reached agreement on all but one matter by June 1952. The remaining issue was the forcible or non-forcible repatriation of prisoners of war. Until that had been solved attacks of varying intensity continued along the Korean battle front. Air and naval combat operations also continued. In April 1953 there were 29,375 effective air sorties, the highest monthly total of the war.

It was during that month that agreement was reached (11 April) to repatriate sick and injured captured personnel; the exchange began on 20 April. Eventually 684 such UN soldiers (including 149 Americans) were freed by the North. The UN Command returned 6,670 Chinese and Koreans to the North. Armistice negotiations resumed on 26 April and continued intermittently until June. On 6 June the negotiators met in Panmunjom, and with only minor points remaining were able to conclude an agreement two days later, guaranteeing voluntary repatriation for anti-communist

prisoners. The next day staff officers started drafting the final cease-fire line.

Comradely assistance in the Korean War.

On 18 June, however, some 25,000 anti-communist North Korean prisoners of war broke out of UN Command prisoner-of-war camps at various places in South Korea. Their release had been ordered by South Korea's president (Syngman Rhee). The North suspended the truce talks indefinitely. A few days later Walter Robertson, President Eisenhower's special truce envoy, held discussions with President Rhee. As a result of these efforts and those of General Clark, negotiations were resumed with the North on 10 July at Panmunjom. Two days later Rhee and Robertson issued a joint statement in which Rhee promised to 'collaborate' in an armistice. Finally, on 27 July the ceremonial signing of the truce documents by General Clark and the representatives of the Chinese people's volunteers and of the North Korean forces took place. It provided for the exchange of prisoners of war and established a two and a half mile demilitarised zone and a demarcation line at the 38th parallel.

On 5 August the first exchange of prisoners – UN and communist – took place at Panmunjom. It was completed on 6 September. By then the UN Command had returned nearly 76,000 prisoners (mostly

North Koreans) to the communists. The North returned almost 13,000 prisoners, most of whom were from South Korea or the USA. There were, however, almost 1,000 British prisoners of war, including Lieutenant J.P. Carne, who had commanded the first battalion, Gloucestershire Regiment, in its stand on the Imjin river in April 1951 and was subsequently awarded the Victoria Cross. The Indian custodial force of five battalions arrived in the demilitarised zone in early September and was involved in further prisoner exchanges.

With the signing of the armistice, the USA implemented pledges to South Korea of a mutual defence treaty and economic assistance. This was formally signed on 1 October, whereby the USA and South Korea would view an armed attack on either as a danger to the other's peace and security. The American Congress authorised some $200 million for the rehabilitation and economic support of the country. Similarly the UN allocated $130 million for its Korean Reconstruction Agency. The Soviet Union and the People's Republic of China provided financial support to North Korea. On 26 October preparatory negotiations for a political conference began at Panmunjom, but little was achieved. On 12 December the talks were temporarily broken off by the UN in protest at communist allegations of 'perfidy' on the part of the United States. Much to the disappointment and frustration of President Rhee, therefore, although the war was over, Korea remained divided. However, the UN Commission for the Unification and Rehabilitation of Korea was not suspended until 1977.

Dag Hammarskjöld.

UNITED NATIONS

The armistice agreement in Korea was seen as a victory for the principle of collective security and raised the status of the UN, which had sixty members throughout 1953. The year opened under the presidency of Lester Pearson, later prime minister of Canada. He was succeeded when the General Assembly reconvened in September by Mme Vijayalakshmi Pandit of India. On 7 April the assembly appointed Dag Hammarskjöld, a Swedish minister of state, as Secretary General and successor to Trygve Lie. The five permanent members of the Security Council were (nationalist)

China, France, the UK, the USA and the USSR. There were six non-permanent members – Chile, Colombia, Denmark, Greece, Lebanon and Pakistan.

The UN dealt with other major political issues besides Korea. These included the question of Palestine and racial segregation in South Africa. There was increasing concern over tension between Israel and its neighbours, Syria and Jordan. The Council took up a Syrian complaint that Israel's diversion of water from the River Jordan for a water-powered project violated the 1949 armistice agreement. The raid on Qibya which had, according to the head of the truce supervision organisation, been carried out by well-trained Israeli soldiers, endangered relations between Jordan and Israel, violating a similar 1949 agreement. The head of the UN Relief and Works Agency for Palestine Refugees in the Near East (UNRWA) reported that there were still 872,000 refugees depending on relief provided by the international community.

The General Assembly also considered the issues arising from South Africa's policies towards the country's majority non-white peoples. In December 1952 the Assembly had established a commission to negotiate a solution in accordance with the UN Charter and the Universal Declaration of Human Rights. In May the country informed the commission that it regarded the Assembly's action as unconstitutional and refused to recognise it. The Assembly was also concerned over racial conflict resulting from South Africa's apartheid policies. The National Party there under Dr Malan was actively intensifying racial segregation and Afrikaner supremacy, having won the General Elections of 1948 and 1953. Much to the

South African apartheid sign.

opposition of the South African member (who saw the issue as an internal matter), the Assembly established another commission to study the racial situation in that country. In its subsequent report it warned that apartheid could only increase the hostile attitude towards whites which was growing under the stimulus of powerful nationalist movements.

Such a situation was indeed already developing. In 1953 the 'M-plan' (a code for Mandela Plan) was established. Under it, leaders of the African National Congress could communicate secretly and quickly by means of an underground network of cells. In September, recognising the difficulties of holding public or trade union meetings to protest against apartheid, Mandela urged people to use other opportunities – over factory machines, in buses and trams – to keep each other informed and ready for action. Above all, in an address to the Transvaal Congress, he stressed that they should *never surrender*.

UNITED STATES OF AMERICA

America had a new President in 1953 – General Dwight ('Ike') Eisenhower. The Vice-President was Richard Nixon; other key members were John Foster Dulles (Secretary of State) and Charles E. Wilson (Secretary of Defence). This was the first Republican administration for twenty-four years. In Congress, given the near-even split between the Republicans and Democrats, Eisenhower's approach was based around a presidential-congressional partnership rather than leadership which his two predecessors had favoured. This was achieved in part through the support of conservative southern Democrats and that of Senator Robert Taft, which ensured Republican support for the President's programme. The death of Taft in July necessitated a more assertive approach by Eisenhower.

Communism was greatly feared in mid-century America in the wake of the Soviet Union's postwar domination of Eastern Europe and the establishment of what was called 'Red China' in 1949. The latter in particular was attributed to communist sympathisers in the outgoing Truman Administration. It was in this atmosphere that the Republican Senator Joseph McCarthy could claim in February 1950 that he had the names of fifty-seven 'card-carrying communists' in the State Department and that over two hundred people employed there were known communist sympathisers. The momentum was to be maintained thereafter, culminating in January 1953 when McCarthy secured the chair of a Senate sub-committee to investigate 'un-American activities' and that of the Senate committee on government operations.

McCarthy used both positions to condemn the previous Truman Administration for treasonable laxity and Eisenhower's for timidity. McCarthy campaigned against what he saw as leftist doctrines encouraged by US Information Service Libraries abroad. He also found fault with the radio station 'Voice of America', and Protestant clergy whom he believed to be 'red-tainted'. The clergy protested to the President, who publicly endorsed their protest as well as defending Allen Welsh Dulles, Director of the Central Intelligence Agency (and brother of the Secretary of State), when McCarthy attacked him. It was against this background that the case of Julius and Ethel Rosenberg came to a climax and once more to international attention.

Allen Dulles, director of the CIA.

The couple, in their mid-thirties, were found guilty of atomic espionage and selling wartime atomic secrets to the Soviet Union. The case evoked widespread concern and protests. There were doubts over the reliability of the evidence of Ethel Rosenberg's brother David Greenglass (himself a spy), who was an important prosecution witness. Also, under American law the death penalty for spying was reserved exclusively for those who committed the offence in wartime. Although the Rosenbergs had passed on the information before the defeat of Germany, their alleged spying was carried out on behalf of a government at the time allied to the United States. Consequently many saw the proposed execution as pandering to the prejudices aroused by McCarthy that dominated the media during the Rosenberg trial. Despite national and worldwide protests (including a plea from the Pope), presidential clemency was refused and the Supreme Court reversed a temporary stay of execution granted on 17 June. The day following was their wedding anniversary, so it was decided that the couple (husband first) should follow each other to the electric chair at Sing Sing prison on 19 June – the first execution carried out in peacetime for espionage in the USA. Jean-Paul Sartre, the French philosopher, writing in *Liberation*, told the American people that they were collectively responsible in either sponsoring or permitting it. 'You allowed the US to become the cradle of a new fascism.' In 1997 a retired KGB officer stated that Julius Rosenberg, although he had helped organise a spy ring, had not been directly involved in stealing atomic secrets and that his wife was not a spy.

The fear of communism continued to dominate and shape American foreign policy in 1953. Therefore it sought to counter Soviet expansion in Europe, the Middle East and the Far East. It hoped to break the stalemate in the Korean truce negotiations. It was also concerned to strengthen its European allies with economic and military aid. Linked with this was its support for European unity, especially through the European Defence Community.

Another fear present in American domestic life related to race. A leading contender for president had championed racial segregation in the 1948 Election. The Supreme Court decision in 1954 on *Brown v the Board of Education of Topeka*, which declared segregation in public schools to be illegal, was an important step towards integration in public institutions. But in March 1953 in Chattanooga, Tennessee, Billy Graham launched the first deliberately integrated Christian mission, tearing down the ropes that separated black and white sections in the stadium there. He was faced with the immediate resignation of the head usher and the subsequent loss of friends as a result. But Graham pressed on, with the active support of Martin Luther King Jr, a pioneer of integration in the divided south.

UNION OF SOVIET SOCIALIST REPUBLICS (USSR)

The death of Stalin in March was the most important single event in the Soviet Union in 1953. He had been the dominant figure in the country since Lenin's death in 1924, and his dictatorship was never challenged. The Soviet people were gradually prepared for the news of his likely demise. At 5 a.m. on 3 March a radio broadcast informed them of the cerebral haemorrhage which he had suffered on the night of 1 March. This had affected vital areas of the brain and thereafter he lost consciousness. Since his heart was healthy and strong, it only gradually affected the breathing centres, in due course causing suffocation and strangulation. He died at 9.50 p.m. Moscow time on 5 March, but this was not announced until 7 a.m.

About 100,000 people assembled to watch the last impressive ceremony in which Stalin's body was laid to rest following the lying-in-state in the Hall of the Columns, House of the Unions, Moscow, 10 March 1953. The coffin-bearers are, from left to right: Shvernik, Kagonovitch, Bulganin, Molotov, Lt Gen Vassily Stalin, son of the late ruler, Malenkov and Beria.

the following day. Thereafter 'every house', according to
contemporary reports, had black-bordered red flags in mourning for
Stalin, and people wept openly in the streets. All foreign embassies
hoisted national flags at half-mast.

Stalin lay in state in an open coffin in the Hall of Columns of the
Dom Soyuzov or Trade Unions House, near the Kremlin, Moscow,
until his funeral on 9 March, at which some forty nations were
represented. Then the coffin was borne by the Russian leaders to a
gun carriage which was drawn by six horses and preceded by a
solitary horseman. The cortège included Stalin's son and daughter.
Malenkov, Beria and Molotov delivered funeral orations. The coffin
was taken into the Mausoleum in Red Square and placed beside that
of Lenin.

The consequences of Stalin's death in terms of personnel and
policy dominated Soviet affairs for most of the rest of 1953.
Malenkov became Chairman of the Council of Ministers (or Prime
Minister) and was supported by a small praesidium consisting of
Beria, Molotov, Kaganovitch and Buganin. Voroshilov became
nominal head of state. Malenkov surrendered his functions as
secretary of the party and Nikita Khrushchev was appointed the
first secretary of the central committee in September, three months
after Beria had been dismissed from the second-highest position in

Mourners waiting to enter the
vast Hall of Columns, where
Stalin's body lay in state in an
open coffin.

the new leadership. Beria was subsequently accused of acting as an agent for the Western powers and promoting the restoration of capitalism in the Soviet Union. In mid-December he was tried in secret by the Soviet Supreme Court, along with six high-ranking officials from the Ministry of Security (which he had once headed). All were found guilty and sentenced to death. There was to be no appeal and the execution was carried out immediately.

Internally there was a slight easing of social and economic restrictions. In foreign affairs there was a more conciliatory attitude towards the non-communist world. On 15 March Malenkov declared that there was in international affairs 'no disputed or unsolved problem which could not be resolved by peaceful means on the basis of mutual understanding between the countries concerned'. This attitude, he added, applied to all countries, including the USA. There were various consequences over the next few months, the most important of which was Soviet support – indeed pressure – for North Korea and the People's Republic of China to conclude the truce which ended the Korean War, but the government did not want to see the area's reunification.

In Europe the German question continued to be the central issue between the Soviet Union and the West. The riots in East Berlin which began on 17 June as an industrial dispute soon widened to a demand for the end of the Soviet-sponsored government of Eastern Germany. Order was re-established with a declaration of martial law and the use of Soviet tanks to repress a workers' rising, resulting in upwards of two hundred dead (no count was taken). The USSR blamed the riots on the American CIA (its chief, Allen Dulles, had been in Berlin the previous week), but at the same time held discussions with the East German government, cancelling war reparations from that area and offering economic concessions which led to lower prices aimed to rebuild the credibility of communism there.

By the end of 1953 Soviet policy seemed to have three main objectives. It wanted to consolidate its influence over Eastern Europe, China and North Korea; to avoid major armed conflict; and to weaken the non-communist world by encouraging disagreement among the Western powers and promoting liberation movements in colonial territories. Generally speaking, such goals were achieved and remained central for the rest of the decade.

FIRST STEPS TOWARDS EUROPEAN UNION

'We must build a kind of United States of Europe. . . . The first step . . . must be a partnership between France and Germany.' This was the heart of a speech which Churchill gave at Zurich in September 1946. The call was to be acted upon within four years and to enjoy some

Robert Schuman, founding father of what was to become the European Union.

success by 1953. Each year since 1945, 8 May had marked the anniversary of the end of the Second World War in Europe. Significantly, Robert Schuman, a former French Prime Minister and at the time Foreign Minister, chose 9 May 1950 to introduce the plan named after him for European integration. He acknowledged that 'Europe will not be created all at once', but proposed that the combined coal and steel production (the materials which had fuelled war between these nations three times in less than eighty years) of France and Germany should be placed under a common, supra-national authority. He saw such a move as 'the first stage in a European federation'.

The European Coal and Steel Community was established under the Treaty of Paris which had been signed in 1951 and came fully into force in 1953. There were six signatories – France, Germany, Italy, Belgium, The Netherlands and Luxembourg. The UK was not a party because although Churchill had been the first postwar leader to speak in terms of a united Europe, he maintained that the Commonwealth and the Special Relationship with the USA were where Britain's interests lay, rather than in Europe. This continued to be the Conservatives' policy in government.

Recognising that personnel as much as materials made for war, another French Prime Minister, René Pleven, had urged a supranational European army in October 1950. This was after several European statesmen, including Churchill, had spoken in favour of a continental army earlier that year. Pleven argued that the battalion should be the largest national unit within the proposed army. Therefore larger fighting forces would of necessity have to be a mix of nationalities. A treaty to establish what was to be known as the European Defence Community (EDC) was signed in Paris in May 1952 by the same six countries which had entered the European Coal and Steel Community. The EDC was defined in the treaty as 'of supranational character with common institutions, common armed forces and a common budget'. Britain (Anthony Eden) and the USA (Dean Acheson) joined in a tripartite declaration with France that any threat to the EDC would be regarded as a threat to their own security.

The British government again supported the venture but declined to join it because of overseas commitments. However, in 1954 the French National Assembly refused, amidst the strains of the *Marseillaise*, to ratify the treaty, and later that year Germany joined NATO. Proposals for a European army effectively died out for the remainder of the twentieth century.

1953: A Year to Remember

THE WEATHER

Apart from the east coast floods at the end of January, generally speaking the weather made little impact on the year. Most districts experienced less rain in the first quarter of the year than in any similar period since 1869, except 1929. Temperatures in these months were below average in England and Wales, but above average in Scotland. April and May were both wetter and sunnier than usual, with Farnham recording a temperature of 89°F on 25 May. It was a cool June and widespread thunderstorms caused much local flooding. Many would later recall

Braving the smog, early 1950s.

how it rained on Coronation Day. August was the warmest month of the year (London recorded a temperature of 93°F on 12 August) and September was fine. Similarly the last quarter of the year was mild, with the country experiencing the driest December for twenty years.

THE EAST COAST FLOODS

For many people the weekend of 31 January–1 February was the most memorable – if most frightening – time of this year. Exceptionally severe gales developed in the Atlantic about 250 miles north-west of the Hebrides on 30 January and within twenty-four hours had moved into the North Sea. By the morning of 31 January gales of up to 113 mph were affecting parts of the country – the highest wind speed to date recorded in Great Britain. The gales swept across Scotland (where a speed of 125 mph was claimed for Costa Head in the Orkneys) and the Irish Sea. Later in the day the depression moved into the western part of the North Sea and huge masses of water were driven southward on to the coasts of eastern England, Belgium and The Netherlands.

Battered by gales for seven hours, the motor-vessel *Princess Victoria*, the Larne–Stranraer mail ferry, sank that day off the coast of County Down. Some 128 people lost their lives. Among those drowned were Major Sinclair, the Northern Ireland Minister of

Queen Elizabeth surveying the damage at Hunstanton with local officials and service personnel, 3 February 1953. (© *Ronald Meek*)

An aerial view of the devastated area around Canvey Island showing the bungalows and houses half submerged by the floods, 2 February 1953.

Finance, and Sir Walter Smiles, MP for North Down at the Westminster Parliament, as well as the Master of the vessel, Captain Ferguson.

In England itself sea-water inundated low-lying land from the Humber to the Thames Estuary. Some fifty miles of the Lincolnshire coast were affected; Mablethorpe and nearby Sutton on Sea were completely flooded, and the entire population had to be evacuated. For the first time ever, in the wake of the River Ouse breaking its bank, a tidal wave some seven feet high swept through the centre of King's Lynn, killing many. Similarly, the sea wall at Hunstanton, Heacham and Snettisham was broken and that at Great Yarmouth much damaged. The River Orwell broke its banks at Felixstowe.

In the Thames Estuary, Canvey Island was flooded, 68 people killed and around 13,000 needed to be evacuated. Buses came from Southend to take people to shelter such as schools in the neighbouring area. The Minister of Food arranged for sweets to be distributed to children in such rest centres. A seventeen-year-old army cadet, while trying to rescue a family by boat, noticed a baby floating by on a door wrenched from its hinges. He dived out of the boat and was injured in a failed rescue attempt. The baby drifted on and was later found dead.

Foulness Island was flooded and Harwich was badly affected too. On reaching the Kent coast, the floods hit Dartford, Gravesend, Herne Bay, Birchington and Margate. Here the harbour lighthouse was destroyed while at Sheerness the naval dockyard was flooded.

The Great Flood rescue of a horse which had been standing in the water for days near Sheerness, Kent, February 1953.

Kent lost thousands of sheep, cattle and horses, and some farmers near Sheerness managed to obtain a rowing boat to rescue their stock, February 1953.

A total of over 300 people died as a result of this catastrophe and some 32,000 people were evacuated. Around 25,000 houses were damaged, with 500 totally destroyed. Similarly some 156,000 acres of agricultural land were flooded (some of it by sea-water), resulting in the loss of several thousand sheep and cattle.

The Queen and the Duke of Edinburgh made separate tours of the flooded areas on 13 February. The Queen visited Tilbury and Purfleet before crossing the Thames by launch to Gravesend and Erith. Throughout her tour she met refugees in rest centres and visited flooded houses. She also attended a special concert to raise funds, given by the London Philharmonic Orchestra at the Royal Albert Hall.

There was an overwhelming response from communities and organisations throughout the country. Wimbledon sent £1,000 and money was also soon received from places as far apart as Birmingham, Exmouth, Lynton and Durham. The St John Ambulance Brigade, the British Red Cross and the Women's Voluntary Service (WVS) all played their part in alleviating distress. The Service revived its wartime 'flying food convoys' to feed people in the flooded areas. Surplus clothing, collected after the Lynmouth disaster of the previous August, with other stocks, had already been distributed to various centres and was available immediately. But more clothing was needed, and soon vans, taxis and cars were queuing to unload clothing for flood victims at the WVS's headquarters at Eaton Square, London.

Parcels of clothing and bedding for those who had suffered were accepted free of charge at all post offices until 17 February, at British Railways and British Road Services and depots. British European Airways did the same for clothing from the Swiss Red Cross. Save the Children Fund, British Columbia, sent some sixty cases of clothing. Those stationed at the American airforce base at Burtonwood, Lancashire, collected toys and household goods for the victims. Some fifteen members of the US airforce and their families at the Hunstanton base had been killed.

The RSPCA rescued some 10,000 animals. These included, in addition to cattle, sheep, horses, pigs, cats and dogs, some 5,000 tame mice, a monkey, three ferrets and five tortoises still in their winter sleep. Bird life was also affected. Bitterns and bearded tits disappeared from Cley on the Norfolk coast because the floods destroyed their breeding places of reed beds. As a result of continuous pumping and dam building, however, the Royal Society for the Protection of Birds was able to lower the level of flood waters in the Society's reserve at Havergate, Suffolk, by March – just in time to allow some avocets, a rare bird last seen in Britain in the mid-nineteenth century, to re-establish their nests.

On 2 February the government promised financial help towards recovery and on the following day the Lord Mayor of London launched a national appeal fund. This had raised £5 million by September, with donations coming from as far away as the USSR, Australia, New Zealand and South Africa. The Anglican Church in Canada gave £20,000 in part to finance emergency repairs to places of worship. The Vatican sent £3,600. The Norwegian government refused payment for the sandbags which it had supplied and made a cash donation too. Finally, having featured in *The Archers*, Ambridge made a contribution of £57 5s to the fund. The money was initially passed to the Lord Mayor of Birmingham. The Lord Mayor of London wrote to the vicar of Ambridge (care of BBC Birmingham studios) to thank the villagers and invited them to call in at Mansion House (his official home) should they ever be nearby so that he might thank them in person.

Britain was not the only country to suffer: in The Netherlands almost 1,800 people were killed and over 100,000 people were evacuated. Even so, this country also contributed to the Lord Mayor's National Flood and Tempest Distress Fund.

A government inquiry was set up in March under Lord Waverley: it reported in the summer and recommended that an early warning system operate on the east coast from mid-September to the end of April. It also recommended that a barrier

Collecting the carcases: the Samson brothers' farm at Iwade, Kent, lost 260 sheep, 30 cows and 2 horses.

be erected across the Thames. Although investigated, this suggestion proved impracticable at the time because of the volume and size of shipping needing access to the Port of London.

Over the same weekend a severe hurricane (upwards of 100 mph) caused considerable damage to forests in north-east Scotland. In the area between Inverness and the River Tay it felled the equivalent of one million tons of timber, most of it Scots pine.

MYXOMATOSIS

This disease had been encouraged in Australia in 1950 to destroy many millions of wild rabbits found in that country. A similar idea was adopted in France in 1952, but the virus, carried by birds and insects, travelled beyond the intended area. A committee, chaired by Lord Carrington (then a junior Minister of Agriculture and later a Conservative Foreign Secretary), was formed to decide policy before disaster struck. But soon afterwards, in October 1953, myxomatosis was found on an estate at Edenbridge, Kent. Rabbit-proof fencing was erected, the rabbits within the area killed and the disease was initially confined to a few hundred acres. However, vets from the Ministry of Agriculture began to inoculate domestic rabbits, especially as there were many thousands of rabbit clubs in Britain at this time. By early November the disease had reached Sussex and before the end of the year Essex and Suffolk as well. Thereafter it continued to spread, killing most wild rabbits within the next two years.

Many farmers were furious that the government initially tried to prevent the spread of a disease which killed this serious pest. Some, it was soon rumoured, deliberately introduced it to their lands because of this. For various reasons the disease aroused a great deal of public interest, but many were warned off this once-popular food source and never ate it again.

BOOKS OF THE YEAR

Dr Alfred Kinsey, author of *Sexual Behaviour in the Human Female*.

One of the most celebrated works of the year was Dr Kinsey's *Sexual Behaviour in the Human Female*. This report, a sequel to one on the human male five years earlier, derived from studies made by his institute in America. Among its conclusions were that almost half of American women had sex before marriage, a quarter were unfaithful afterwards and that a quarter of those unmarried had a female homosexual relationship. The report had a mixed reception both in the UK and in America. Critics argued that its sampling procedures were poor, being more indicative of college-educated middle-class mid-western women who adhered to few current orthodox religious

views, and that the institute's interviewing techniques were open to serious error. Simone de Beauvoir's *The Second Sex*, a pioneering work putting sex as experienced by the woman into a historical and political context, appeared in translation in 1953.

Children's author Enid Blyton signing autographs for eager schoolboys, London, 7 January 1953.

The most successful British female writers in 1953 included Georgette Heyer (whose *Cotillion* appeared this year), Barbara Cartland (*Cupid Rides Pillion*; *Love Me Forever*) and Agatha Christie whose detective novels this year included *A Pocketful of Rye* and a play, *Witness for the Prosecution*, which opened in October and was an expanded version of an earlier short story.

Enid Blyton was the bestselling children's author. In 1953, as before, the 'Famous Five' and 'Secret Seven' sold well, as did Blyton's compilations of Bible stories and *The Story of Our Queen*. But it was Noddy who enjoyed the greatest success. He, along with Big Ears the pixie, teddy bears Mr and Mrs Tubby and PC Plod, among others, had first appeared in 1949 with *Little Noddy Goes to Toytown*. The huge impact of Noddy was in part due to the accompanying

HERE COMES LITTLE NODDY... by Enid Blyton

802.—"I **must** have my clothes," said Noddy. "I'm cold." "Well, you can't put on wet clothes," said Roundy. "Hey, clown, can you lend Noddy some dry clothes?"

803.—"Of course," said the clown that Roundy had wound up. "Half a minute, I live near by. I'll get a suit for him." And he disappeared into a little house.

804.—He came out again with a small gay suit and held it out. "Oh!" cried Noddy, in delight. "It's a CLOWN'S suit! Oh, Roundy, shall I put it on?"

(To be continued to-morrow)·

The *Evening Standard*, 16 June 1953.

illustrations by the Dutch artist Harmsen Van Der Beek. By 1953 Noddy featured in a cartoon strip in the London *Evening Standard* (later collated to form strip books) which was also illustrated by Van Der Beek, who died during the course of the year. Robert Tyndall was his successor. Blyton had by then produced eight Noddy books with total sales of 10 million. With the aid of a 'Noddy dictionary' prepared by the publishers, however, other artists could continue to illustrate the works in the same style. The dictionary defined the Toyland characters and included an annotated map. Soon manufacturers used it too, marketing for example 'Noddy' toys, games, soap, clothing and pottery. The character also appeared on cereal packets and biscuit boxes. The first Noddy pantomime was produced in 1954. Tyndall provided the necessary drawings for such promotions and entertainments.

Captain W.E. Johns was still writing Biggles books, which were aimed at boys. He also wrote about Worrals of the Women's Auxiliary Air Force (WAAF) for girls, originally devised as a heroine to encourage young girls to enlist in the services during the Second World War.

In the wake of the continuing development and display of nuclear weaponry, it was not surprising that this, too, featured in the literature of the time. In 1953 John Wyndham's *The Kraken Wakes* appeared. The title is from Tennyson's poem about a mysterious, sleeping, undersea monster whom no human has seen. In Wyndham's novel, the Kraken, having been woken by nuclear explosions, acquires atomic weapons. This results in melting ice caps and the flooding out of the human race. Someone able to save the world from various dangers and named after an ornithologist also made his appearance in 1953 – James Bond in *Casino Royale*. However, the first Bond novel made little initial impact, selling fewer than 8,000 copies in twelve months.

Works about life overseas included Freya Stark's *The Coast of Incense*. The third volume of her autobiography, it told of her travels in Southern Arabia in the 1930s. E.M. Forster's novel *The Hill of Devi* concerned a central Indian state and its ruling maharaja, while Heinrich Harrier's saga of his escape from an Indian prison camp to become educator and adviser to the Dalai Lama and his court was also well received under its English title, *Seven Years in Tibet*. But the most-read work about the Indian continent was Sir John Hunt's *Ascent of Everest*, the profits of which funded the Mount Everest Foundation which encouraged research into mountain regions worldwide. At the earth's other extreme was Jacques Cousteau's *The Silent World*, an amazing account of the ocean bed. Three years earlier he had been made commander of the oceanographic ship *Calypso*, from which he made the first underwater film.

Other works to appear this year included L.P. Hartley's *The Go-Between* and Evelyn Waugh's *Love Among the Ruins*, a satire similar to Huxley's *Brave New World*. J.B. Priestley wrote *The Other Place*, and Rosamond Lehmann *The Echoing Grove*, while C.S. Forester added to the 'Hornblower' series with *Hornblower and the Atropos*. John Wain wrote *Hurry on Down*, a novel soon to be associated with the cultural label 'Anger', a mood which came to wider attention the following year with Kingsley Amis's novel *Lucky Jim*.

Poetry by Robert Graves, Cecil Day Lewis, Edith Sitwell and Walter De La Mare was published, and there were poetry prizes for Dylan Thomas (who died in 1953), Edwin Muir, Elizabeth Jennings and Kathleen Raine. Dorothy Hewlett's biography of Elizabeth Barrett Browning led to a revival of interest in this poet's work.

THEATRE

Perhaps the most significant work of the year was T.S. Eliot's *The Confidential Clerk*. This play, like the writer's previous, *The Cocktail Party*, was originally produced in Edinburgh during the Festival in August. It opened in London the following month to great acclaim. It starred Denholm Elliott (as Colby Simpkins) and Margaret Leighton (Lucasta Angel). Eliot's *Murder in the Cathedral* was staged at the Old Vic in March, making a contrast with its original place of production, the precincts of Canterbury Cathedral, and presenting

Ernest Hemingway and his wife, Mrs Leland Hayward, actor Spencer Tracy, producer/actor George Jessel, and theatre/television/screen producer Leland Hayward, all enjoying dinner and a chat at a New York night club, including negotiations of making a film from Hemingway's Nobel Prize winning book *The Old Man and the Sea*, 30 June 1953.

the opportunity for a more energetic rendering than that hallowed setting had allowed.

R.C. Sherriff, who had enjoyed such success with *Journey's End* (1929), with its subject of life in the trenches of the First World War, now turned to the home front and the aftermath of the Second World War with *The White Carnation*. The play was set in a house haunted by the earth-bound spirit of a man killed in an air-raid. There is a mixture of styles: the serious, a soul doomed to expiate wrongs committed during his lifetime; and the comic, given the problems local authority staff face in dealing with a person who does not officially exist. Some critics thought the subject needed a more sober approach. *The Bad Samaritan* by William Douglas Home was viewed in a similar way.

The Shakespeare Memorial Trust had a particularly successful season. It opened in March with *The Merchant of Venice*, starring Michael Redgrave (as Shylock) and Peggy Ashcroft (Portia). Later in the season both took the lead in *Antony and Cleopatra* and brought the play to London in November. With an eye to the coronation, the

Old Vic put on *King Henry VIII*. The speeches in praise of another Elizabeth and its scenes showing Londoners preparing for a coronation were deemed (rightly) to have popular appeal. The Queen herself attended a performance and the theatre was open on 2 June itself. The Birmingham Repertory Theatre Company made history by producing all three parts of *King Henry VI* as an integrated whole. Bernard Miles's mobile Elizabethan theatre, the Mermaid, staged a series of plays and an opera.

Other revivals worthy of note were Shaw's *The Apple Cart* and *Pygmalion*, as well as Donald Wolfit's production of the two Oedipus plays of Sophocles. There were also Sir John Gielgud's productions of William Congreve's *Way of the World* and Thomas Otway's *Venice Preserv'd* (Paul Scofield played Pierre), which is often regarded as this late seventeenth-century dramatist's best work.

Plays by contemporary dramatists included *A Day by the Sea* (N.C. Hunter) and *The Living Room*, Graham Greene's first play. The Hunter work starred Ralph Richardson, Sybil Thorndike, Megs Jenkins and Irene Worth. John Gielgud starred and directed in what was described by its enthusiasts as 'English seaside Chekov'; Kenneth Tynan viewed it as 'an evening of unexampled triviality'. It enjoyed some success but was rarely to be revived thereafter. *The Living Room* featured Dorothy Tutin, Eric Portman and Mary Jerrold. It was a dark tale of a Catholic household imprisoned within itself. It comprised three elderly people and a young girl, their niece. The girl, perhaps desperate to escape, had fallen in love with a middle-aged married man. She later committed suicide, in part because of her own sense of sin but also because of her fanatically religious aunts.

On a lighter note there was Kenneth Horne in *Trial and Error* and *Airs on a Shoestring*, which saw the long-derelict Royal Court Theatre vibrant once more. Other popular shows were the Crazy Gang's *Ring out the Bells* and two American musicals. *Guys and Dolls* opened on 28 May in London after playing in New York since November 1950. It ran for over a year (555 performances) at the Coliseum. *The King and I* began its long run (926 performances) at the Theatre Royal, Drury Lane, on 8 October. The lead players were Valerie Hobson (as the widowed Anna Leonowens) and Herbert Lom (the King of Siam).

SCIENTIFIC DISCOVERIES AND MEDICAL ACHIEVEMENTS

Perhaps the most significant scientific publication of the year was a 900-word paper entitled 'The Molecular Structure of Nucleic Acids', which appeared in *Nature* on 25 April. It can be said to have created

Crick and Watson's DNA molecular model, 1953. This DNA (deoxyribose nucleic acid) model contains the metal plates used by Francis Crick and James Dewey Watson to determine the molecular structure of DNA. It is constructed out of metal plates and rods arranged helically around a retort stand, and shows one complete turn of the famous double helix. The metal plates represent the four bases whose complementary arrangement immediately suggested a possible copying mechanism for the genetic material.

the science of molecular biology. Its authors were Francis Crick and James Dewey Watson.

Crick, born in Northampton and a graduate of London University, only became interested in chemical research in 1946 although he was also influenced by Erwin Schrödinger's *What is Life?* and its suggestion that quantum mechanics might be applied to genetics. In 1949 he began to work for the Cambridge Medical Research Council Unit at the Cavendish Laboratory. In 1951 he was joined there by an American, James Watson, who had also read *What is Life?* while a zoology student at the University of Chicago. This led him to the study of microbiology. On a visit to Europe, Watson met Maurice Wilkins, who ran the biophysics unit at King's College, University of London, and specialised in X-ray diffraction pictures of DNA. He showed some of the results to Watson who thereupon decided that he would attempt to discover the structure of DNA, realising that this would enable molecular biology to advance and with it the science of genetic engineering.

Although the Cavendish Laboratory had an informal agreement with King's that only the latter would study DNA, Crick and Watson collaborated to work unofficially in this area. Although King's was unaware of this, Watson was invited to a seminar given by Rosalind Franklin, outlining her work in X-ray diffraction. She in turn was invited to comment on a triple-helix structure which Crick and Watson had devised at Cambridge. She found many shortcomings. Furthermore, in 1953 they acquired details of a DNA model constructed at King's. But this too was inadequate and included errors similar to those identified by Franklin. Crick and Watson gradually realised how the King's College model might be put right, especially as Franklin's latest work in crystallography had given much better pictures of DNA and with it more accurate measures of its dimensions. The breakthrough came when Watson realised that he was using the wrong isomeric form of the bases, that the bases fitted together on the inside to form the perfect double-helix structure. The work explained how DNA is capable of transmitting hereditary traits in living organisms.

Colleagues were told of this in early March, and the world six weeks later. Franklin accepted the model. In 1962 Watson, Crick and Wilkins were awarded the Nobel Prize for Medicine. The Nobel Prize only goes to living recipients and can only be shared among three winners. Rosalind Franklin received nothing, having died four years earlier of cancer.

An American, Dr J.H. Gibbon, performed the first successful open-heart surgery. The patient was Cecelia Bavolek. Her blood was artificially circulated and oxygenated by a heart-lung machine. It was in this year too that the first Siamese twins were separated successfully and the American physiologist Ancel Keys suggested the link between heart diseases and high-fat diet. There were also major advances in tackling polio as a result of the work of Dr Jonas Salk of the University of Pittsburgh. He reported the success of the polio vaccine in January, following a series of preliminary tests on 600 people including himself, his wife and children. Soon began a massive trial involving nearly two million children. Finally Frederick Sanger became the first person to determine the structure of a protein – insulin.

1953 NOBEL PRIZEWINNERS

Alfred Nobel, a Swedish chemist and engineer, established the Nobel Foundation. The first prizes were awarded in 1901 for chemistry, physics, medicine, literature and peace. The value of each prize in 1953 was about £12,000.

The Nobel prize for chemistry was won by Hermann Staudinger, a German scientist and retired professor of Freiburg University for his study of polymers. He discovered a way to synthesise fibre, a key to the development of the modern plastics industry. The physics prize went to a Dutch scientist, Professor Frits Zernicke, who had pioneered a special microscope which could see living cells that had been coloured by light waves. It was to be used in cancer research. That for medicine was shared by two German-born biochemists – Fritz Albert Lipman and Hans Adolphe Krebs. The former was by this

Alfred Nobel.

Albert Schweitzer, winner of the Nobel Peace Prize.

time at Harvard Medical School, while Professor Krebs was at Sheffield University. Although they worked independently, the citation referred to their work on the processes carried on within human cells.

No peace prize had been awarded in 1952. It was announced in the autumn of 1953 that it would go to Dr Albert Schweitzer, the celebrated Christian theologian, musician and medical missionary. He was 'deeply happy' about accepting the prize but, because he was so busy, could not receive it until his visit to Europe in 1954. The prize money was used to establish a village for 250 lepers next to his hospital at Lambarene, a missionary station on the Ogowe river in The Gabon, which was then part of French Equatorial Africa. The 1953 peace prize winner was George Marshall. Although he had been a key figure in the plan for the invasion of France in 1944 ('Operation Overlord'), he was more renowned now for the American financial help to postwar Europe, 'Marshall Aid'.

Churchill was given the award for literature, but admitted that he would have preferred to have won the Nobel peace prize. Indeed, he was unable to attend the ceremony in December because he was returning from the disappointing Bermuda Conference, which he had hoped would offer a path to peace. The prize instead was for his writings and wartime speeches, the citation referring to 'his mastery of historical and biographical description as well as for the brilliant art of oration with which he defended high human values'. This was the first time the enduring quality of the spoken word had been so honoured. Many people wrote to congratulate Churchill – including his bank manager on the day the £12,093 was deposited into the Prime Minister's account.

HERITAGE

Heritage was a major theme of 1953. At the end of July, in the wake of the Gowers Report, the Historic Buildings and Ancient Monuments Bill became law. Under this legislation three historic building councils were established in England, Wales and Scotland. Grants were available to owners, local authorities and the National Trust for the preservation of historic buildings, contents and landscape settings. Local authorities and the National Trust (and the then Ministry of Works) were further empowered to make purchases in accordance with set criteria.

The National Trust, founded in 1895, saw its membership increase from 36,000 to 44,500 and gain responsibility for a further nine properties, including Lanhydrock in Cornwall and Nymans Gardens in Sussex. The gardens were already celebrated for their hydrangeas, rhododendrons, magnolias, rare trees and plants.

Especially in coronation year, Westminster Abbey was conscious of its long history and role in the nation's affairs. But equally those in charge were also acutely aware that much needed to be done to safeguard the building to ensure its future. Consequently a £1 million appeal was launched at the end of January in the Jerusalem Chamber, as the main abbey was closed in preparation for the coronation. The first gift was from the Queen and the royal family. Some £900,000 had been received by the end of the year. It was to be spent in part on maintenance and the abbey choir school. Such support derived from various sources, including a production of Christopher Hassell's *Out of the Whirlwind*, performed in the abbey itself.

Significantly too, 1953 was the first full year of the Historic Churches Preservation Trust. It had been founded in September 1952 in response to a Church (of England) Assembly Report that £4 million was needed over the following ten years to repair Anglican places of worship. The Queen became its patron and its first trustees, in addition to leading church figures, included Churchill, Attlee, the Lord Chancellor, the Speaker of the House of Commons, the Governor of the Bank of England and the TUC chairman. A public appeal was launched in London on 1 December 1952. Seven runners, all former Oxford Blues or Olympic competitors, carried a dispatch box containing the Lord Mayor's gift in relays from the Mansion House to St Martin-in-the-Fields. Other gifts followed quickly, ranging from 2*s* 6*d* to £5,000 (the latter from the Bank of England). The Pilgrim Trust was also generous (£100,000 over ten years), and overseas donations came from, among other places, Italy, Belgium, Switzerland, Singapore, South Africa, Canada and the United States. But local fund-raising also mattered. A collecting box, appropriately enough in the form of a church, was designed. This cost 1*s* 6*d* and was highly commended in the British Paper Box Design Contest. The Trust was also featured in the BBC programme *The Week's Good Cause* in July, raising £4,800. During 1953 some 143 Anglican and seven Nonconformist churches were offered grants by the Trust.

CHRISTMAS PREPARATIONS

Christmas decorations often began to appear in early December in the shops, public houses and hotels. Many homes waited until later in the month, some only buying and decorating the Christmas tree on the last day before the great event. The fountains and Norwegian Christmas tree in Trafalgar Square were not illuminated until 19 December – both sets of lights that day were on from late afternoon until 11 p.m. This was not normally so: because of energy implications, they might overlap for less than two hours. Longer hours operated, however, over the three days of Christmas and New Year's Eve (until 12.15 a.m. on the latter occasion). Carols were sung around the tree twice nightly and in the last days before Christmas the Bach Choir and that of the People's Dispensary for Sick Animals were among those who performed.

Announcements for the festive occasion were also made at that time, in particular postal arrangements and travel. In 1953 Christmas Day was on a Friday. The last dates for sending greetings cards to mainland Europe was 12 December and within the UK the 21st. Post was to be delivered on Christmas Day but not on the following two days in England and Wales; normal postal services operated in Scotland on both Christmas and Boxing Day. Some 130,000 extra but temporary staff were recruited, mostly from among university students. Cheap long-distance telephone ('trunk') calls were suspended on the evenings of 24–26 December.

British Railways ran extra trains in England on Christmas Eve and a Sunday service on Christmas Day itself. It offered fewer trains than a Sunday on Boxing Day but more than usual on the day after. The reduced-price early-morning, shift workers' and cheap weekend tickets continued to be available. There was a normal rail service in Scotland throughout the Christmas period, with additional trains operating between the two countries on selected days. Public houses could open for longer. On Christmas Eve they could close at 11.15 p.m.

Young television viewers, early 1950s.

CHRISTMAS GOODS, 1953

Toaster	£2 2s
Anglepoise lamp	£4 14s 8d
Wolf Cub electric drill	£5 19s 6d
Plate warmer	£2 15s
Bed-warming pans	£2 14s 4d
Ormond hair dryer	£3 8s 10d
Philishave razor	£6 12s 2d
Sprouts	4d per pound
Cabbage and savoy	3d per pound
Celery	6d–1s per head
Cockles	1s per half-pint
Winkles	1s per pint
Mandarins	2d each
South African oranges	7 for 1s
Grapes	1s 9d–2s 3d per pound
Tunisian dates	1s 9d–2s 6d per box
Greek figs	10d per box
Turkish figs	1s per box

Christmas clubs normally paid out from about mid-December. Rising prosperity and only minimal rationing still in force meant that most retailers had a particularly good Christmas. Although butter was still scarce, sugar and dried fruit were readily available, so more women now made their own cakes and could ice them generously. There was a good supply, too, of turkeys and chickens, which made for wonderful shop-window displays on a scale not seen since before the war. Above all, there was a big demand for cheap wine following a glut in France and Portugal.

Electrical goods were much in demand, especially the cream or grey Morphy-Richards hairdryer (model H1) launched earlier that year and the Russell Hobbs tea-maker (model TM1), which had also just been introduced. But home-crafted presents were popular this year too, especially basketry, canework and jewellery; evening institutes offered classes for people to learn the skills. Nylon stockings (now more readily available) were often given, as were bath sets – 'Freesia' by Yardley was popular and comprised two bars of soap, three bath-salt cubes and a tin of talcum powder. Lipstick was another frequent gift, sales having been boosted by the technicolor films released earlier in the year.

CHRISTMAS DAY: CARE IN THE COMMUNITY

Concern for the elderly and lonely was very much in evidence. The Mayor visited Epsom hospitals and the elderly at home and in

Christmas shopping, 1950s.

institutions with presents of cakes, sweets, toys and cigarettes. At Epsom Cottage Hospital every ward had a tree and every patient awoke to find a full sock at the end of the bed. The long-established Epsom Parochial Charities, which were responsible for the local almshouses, distributed around one hundred tons of coal to the old and needy.

THE QUEEN'S CHRISTMAS BROADCAST

The Queen made a radio broadcast from Auckland, New Zealand, the first royal Christmas message to have been given from outside Britain. It was preceded by a programme entitled *The Queen's Journey*, which was a combined effort involving the Australian, New Zealand and British broadcasting organisations. It opened with a Maori haka from Rotorua, there were tributes from British territories and former colonies, and the programme ended with 1953's most celebrated New Zealander, Sir Edmund Hillary, giving the Commonwealth's greeting to the Queen from his sister's home near Sandringham. The Queen's message itself was broadcast at 9 a.m. GMT (9 p.m. New Zealand time) and sent by land-line to Wellington then by radio-telephone directly to the UK via Sydney and Barbados. It was also transmitted from Sydney via the British Far Eastern Broadcasting Service in Malaya. The message was re-broadcast from London at 3 p.m. but, specifically at the Queen's request, only on radio. For many it remained a high point of the festive day and a reminder of the way in which she had shaped and dominated the most memorable event of 1953. But for others, life was only just beginning . . .

PEOPLE BORN IN 1953

11 January	John Sessions
6 May	Tony Blair
16 May	Pierce Brosnan
19 May	Victoria Wood
8 June	Bonnie Tyler
6 November	Griff Rhys Jones
8 December	Kim Basinger
9 December	John Malkovich

Waiting for Father Christmas: children at a Dr Barnardo's home hanging up their stockings.

INDEX